AFTERSHOCKS: CONTEMPORARY SYRIAN PROSE

McSWEENEY'S 76

COVER PHOTO: Hrair Sarkissian.

INTERIOR ILLUSTRATIONS: Anuj Shrestha.

Printed in Canada

This project is supported in part by the National Endowment for the Arts.
To find out more about how National Endowment for the Arts grants
impact individuals and communities, visit www.arts.gov.

DEAR MCSWEENEY'S,
I send you my greetings carried
by doves and perfumed by love,
sea salt, and rosemary like the mix
I smelled when I arrived at dawn
in Beirut last summer. It was the
first time I crossed the ocean after
six years of living in Las Vegas
Valley and being unable to travel,
waiting for Homeland Security to
accept and approve my status as a
new legal alien.

I stood at the Lebanese passport check-in, my eyes tracing
Arabic script on signs and ads.
It felt familiar and strange—was
it because I had not seen Arabic
letters in public signs in years,
or was it the charm of Lebanese
calligraphy? The old software of
my mind was being updated as
I listened to people around me
speaking Arabic. By the time
I was in the taxi, I was talking
nonstop, mixing Egyptian dialect
with what I still remember of the
Levant dialect. I thirsted—to hear
it, to see the script in its rightful
form, not scattered letters as I saw
it, printed wrongly most of the
time, in AMERIKA.

On my first night in Beirut,
I searched for what I missed most:
Arabic art and culture events.
I went to the Madina Theater,
and upon entering, I was surprised to see it transformed into
an art gallery; the rows of chairs
had been removed to create small
enclosed spaces. These intimate
rooms allowed for a unique
experience, where only one visitor
at a time could enter to view the
paintings. Accompanying the
visuals, moaning and hissing
sounds emerged from the shadows.
The exhibition was titled *Sleeping
Tongues*. In the paintings, I saw
bodies wrapped over each other in
after-sex laziness or dreamy awakening. Erotic electrification was
flickering in the theater darkness.
Afterward, there was a public
discussion featuring two art critics
and the artist. I sat there with a
childish grin, unable to believe
how much I had missed this; a
fiery rose sprouted in my stomach.
My past life as an Arabic writer
is behind me; in the last couple
of years, I submerged myself in
English, crafting a new face for
an exiled, immigrant writer who
looks to the future. Still, it was
charming visiting the past.

Suddenly, a gentleman to my
side asked, "Are you Ahmed Naji?"

I am Ahmed Naji, so I said
yes and shook his hand. He was a
journalist whose works I had read
before. Another person said hi;
she followed me on Twitter and
had read some of my writing. My
cheeks turned red, and a mix of

shyness and excitement engulfed me. I was happy to be in a place where I was known through my writing, not through my explanation; I was flattered and felt like a celebrity. Drinks followed their greetings, and yes, in theaters and art galleries in Beirut, there are full bars where you can get amazing cocktails that cost less than seven dollars.

Afterward, we went to a bar and a restaurant, where again I enjoyed my little fame when the owner welcomed me. He asked how long I was staying and suggested hosting a reading event or book signing for my latest Arabic novel. I apologized and told him I was there to meet and listen to people and wasn't sure if I had anything valuable to share. I added, "I feel like I've even forgotten how to tell a joke in Arabic."

For the next couple of days, I indulged in Beirut pleasures. I went to the mountains, walked by the sea, and danced until morning at a live Palestinian rap concert featuring artists banned from the US. I ate nonstop all the food that I missed, trying for the first time raw ground lamb meat and liver with lemon and onion. Day and night, I drank arak.

Arak was the first alcoholic drink I ever tried when I was young, but it's rare in Las Vegas. In the last six years, I could find only three bottles. Known by various names, arak is considered the king of Mediterranean spirits. It is distilled from grapes and aniseed. Sometimes, dates or figs are added. Arak is colorless, but you don't drink it neat; instead, you add water and watch the metamorphosis as its color changes to milky white. You can enjoy it with food as an appetizer or at night while dancing or during intense political debates.

Due to jetlag, I found myself awake before sunrise, standing on the balcony, gazing at the Beirut sea. I listened to the call to prayer—another thing I missed—and I watched the city awaken, slowly drifting toward the unknown.

Even the present feels uncertain; ambiguity is Lebanese business. I wandered the streets, tracing the scars of destruction/defacement on the city's buildings. I wondered whether these marks are from the civil war or the Israeli war in 2006 or the Beirut harbor explosion or the last failed revolution.

I met Fawwaz Traboulsi, a writer and historian whose work has profoundly influenced me; we have exchanged emails for years. During the summer, he resides in the mountains to escape the unbearable humidity of Beirut, but he came down to meet me for lunch. Fawwaz is a Marxist who was actively involved with the Lebanese communist party during the Lebanese Civil War and the Israeli invasion of Lebanon in the eighties. He also played a role in the social movements in southern Yemen, earned his PhD in history in the eighties, and has taught at New York University and the American University of Beirut. He is the author of several books and Edward Said's Arabic translator; now eighty-three years old, he maintains a robust physique and a sharp mind. He teased me when I apologized for not drinking arak at lunch at 1 p.m.; thus, I ended up joining him. In the middle of the conversation, he told me that the current days are worse than during the civil war. Surprised, I responded, "It's certainly tough now, but worse than the war days?" He replied, "Absolutely, it was a proxy war. Then, unlike now, money flowed freely into the country."

Now, only one party controls the country with a coalition of short-sighted political parties. For more about this issue, dear McSweeney's, I recommend checking the English-language site Megaphone: The Voice of Lebanon's Uprising. More importantly, I want you to know that Beirut's shore is rocky, so there are few sandy beaches, but you can go to "sea clubs" where one can savor seafood meals while seated beside the sea. Here, swimming pools are constructed on the rocks, allowing you to swim with sea views. Children run and laugh, young lovers in swimsuits kiss in the shade, and families take boat tours through Beirut's sea caves. Those are the images Beirut left printed on my memory.

Back home in Las Vegas, the American Homeland Security officer at the airport, as usual, stopped me and searched my bags. He looked at my papers and found that he and I lived in the same neighborhood; we joked about how the construction that was going on in Charleston was taking forever. He grabbed his clipboard and explained that because I was coming from Lebanon, he had to ask me several questions for his "form." The first question was "Have you ever been to any Hezbollah territory?" I smiled at him and said, "Well, you know, Hezbollah is currently ruling the country, so I'm not sure what 'their territory' means." He shook his head and said, "Me neither. This form is not updated, but we have to follow the formula."

I am writing to memorialize this short visit because I fear it might get wiped from my memory. Now I wake up to images and news of the genocide in Gaza; then I check in on my friends in Lebanon while an Israeli American aircraft flew above them and an Israeli "philosopher," Yuval Harari, threatened to nuke Lebanon.

Oh, dear McSweeney's, I wish to find arak soon in Vegas; we all need to swim in the dreamy clouds to continue living through such hellish times.

Best,

AHMED NAJI
LAS VEGAS, NEVADA

DEAR MCSWEENEY'S,

Before Al and I went to Los Angeles, there was an earthquake in New York City. It feels, I think, a little silly to call it that, a thing of such magnitude that it couldn't even set off a car alarm. We were going to Los Angeles because of all that is happening with Al's incredible novel. Soon after the quake, depending on whether you measure time by how it passes or by how it feels like it passes, we were in the air. I do not know that

I have ever been able to measure a thing other than by how I perceive it. Flying to California from New York City is a wild thing. You get up around seven for a flight around nine and arrive, nearly six hours later, around noon. The sky is clear and bright, and you get to your hotel and spend a lot of time by the pool, writing, staring up at the hills and the observatory, watching the palm trees sway taller than any building between you and the hills, like long-standing monuments to a city that lives only in our communal dreams.

It's nice to deploy a little second person plural to make grand sweeping statements as a defense against intimacy. Nearly all of my vacations have involved my family. The ones Al and I take, just us, feel so precious to me. I count the seconds of vacation like I count the seconds at my job; when I am at work I count out how every second of my life is being sold to pay for time down the road, and when I am on vacation, I can see that clock rolling back with each purchase, each step, each glance, each ride, each breath. We live in a nation that built itself on the idea that all things can be bought and sold. It is so beautiful here in Los Angeles in the sun that I would like to cry. My eyes are so full

I can hardly see. I blink. I stare at the hills through my sunglass clip-ons that are gray, which I believe helps with my colorblindness, which has gotten a little worse as I age, like my hairline and my hearing and my spine, and then I think about the way I have paid for all these things and the costs they carry and my eyes find the observatory and I think about the stars and feel glad I bought the clip-ons, that I can still turn my head. "Even in summer I miss summer" is an incredible line I never could have written and which I think about every day, its author a wonder whom I may never speak to again. Especially on vacation I wish I was on vacation. Everything has a cost here. The lights, the air, the plane, the pool, the food that is brought to us on plates on a tray by the pool and in bed, the death we rain down on all the world. To not think about this is a gift and to pretend it doesn't exist is a kind of death I do not wish to die. The water of the pool was calm and the sky was blue and bright. In Los Angeles we wrote and we ate and we moved around the town, we caught a ball game, we met people, we ate, we wrote, we moved around the town some more, we came home by the light of the moon, our eyes red.

A red-eye cooks your brain like nothing else. I got up and got off the plane and opened the door to our apartment, where I opened up my laptop and went to work as best I could. What a world this is, where a few of us can get jobs that let us work from almost anywhere. I struggle with how beautiful this life I have is. I am not used to thinking my life is a beautiful thing. To hold both ideas in my hands has been a hard one. May it always be this way. The land shifts, the sky shifts, our hearts and our minds shift. The only thing true here is what ground we can stand on. I hope this letter finds you well.

All my love,

SASHA FLETCHER
BROOKLYN, NEW YORK

DEAR MCSWEENEY'S,
I am an American Peace Corps volunteer co-teaching an English as a foreign language (EFL) class with my Mexican counterpart. Many EFL teachers are trained to believe students learn best with repeated grammar drills, and short reading and listening activities about unrelatable things like an American tourist's vacation itinerary in Paris. It's no wonder many students are not excited about English.

But this class I am co-teaching is not a traditional EFL class, and my co-teacher, Paloma de Jesus Luqueño Falcon, is no ordinary English teacher. Paloma demands more from her students than most teachers do. Coincidentally, her name reflects her teaching style. Like a dove, she radiates peace and calm. But when needed, she becomes a keen-eyed raptor circling from above, looking to pull out the best bits of her students no matter how uncomfortable that process may be.

She is petite—five foot, one inch—a hugger who is quick to smile. Her respect for her job and her students is reflected in the way she dresses. Flawless makeup and nails, and coordinated outfits. She is partial to jewelry made of healing crystals. There is an Earth Mother aura that radiates from her. So much so that it surprises me to see those moments when the falcon is on full display.

She is also a fighter, a *chambeadora*. In addition to teaching, she sells clothing, shoes, and jewelry. She is the best-stocked teacher I have ever met. In her tiny, neat office anything you could ever want is tucked away in some crevice. Need markers? Candy? Playing cards? Pliers? A piece of obsidian? Paloma magically whips whatever you need out of a drawer. She is so well stocked that I have taken to calling her Señorita Amazon. She brings that same level of hustle, creativity, and drive to her classroom.

When a nursing student refuses to participate, Paloma does not retreat. She advances. Today, Paloma and I are teaching an activity we cocreated with my Peace Corps supervisor called Acquiring Cross Cultural and English Skills for Success (ACCESS).

Our ACCESS classes are bilingual and bicultural, and they focus predominantly on imparting a better understanding of US culture. Our students are free to express themselves in either Spanish or English. Each class has a theme that our students can engage with deeply. Some of our past classes focused on Black American history, which brought up discussions of inequality and colorism in Mexico. We did a Native American heritage class that tied back into the Indigenous experience in Mexico. The rich and relatable subject matter often gets students to loosen their reluctance to participate. In these classes, students are eager to share their thoughts and opinions.

The classes move quickly and utilize lots of multimedia. Music, videos, quizzes, and group discussions keep our students engaged throughout. Each session requires students to tap into their emotional intelligence and critical-thinking skills. The subject matter takes center stage, while the English is allowed to ebb and flow. All students get invaluable exposure to a native speaker sharing comprehensible and relatable content. Paloma translates as needed.

Co-teaching these classes has been emotionally taxing not just for our students but for us as well. The most emotional discussions always follow an exercise in which we separate the class based on which gender they identify as and ask the question "What is the hardest part of being a woman in Mexico?" I have co-taught this class thirty-one times, with twelve different co-teachers to over seven hundred students, and when this question is asked, invariably the answer is "Inseguridad!"

I was shocked and overwhelmed with emotion the first time I heard my young female students talk about feeling unsafe. Specific and broad answers to this question pour out of young women as if they have been waiting years for this question to be asked. Our students always seem relieved to be in a space where they can speak their truth without fear of being silenced or mocked.

Teaching these sessions has revealed that English classes don't have to be superficial and unrelatable. They can be a forum for sharing, healing, and connection not just for our students but for teachers as well.

My only regret is that I did not share my gratitude to my students for their willingness to process such profound and personal feelings in my presence. These moments with Paloma and my eleven other co-teachers, and especially my students, are precious to me. While teaching, I was given many gifts: mutual understanding, genuine friendship, and belonging.

Sincerely,

MARY WILLIAMS
LOS ANGELES, CALIFORNIA

INTRODUCTION

by ALIA MALEK

BY THE TIME THE 2023 earthquake struck Syria and Turkey—where nearly four million Syrian refugees live—Syrians had already survived many a metaphorical tremor.

There was the dictatorship—corrupt, violent, deadly, and decades long, which kept the country and its people mired in a seemingly forever present. With the 2011 Arab Spring, the momentum of the future seemed unstoppable, and hope was high that the era of dictators would be soon relegated to the past. But the regime met the people's demands with violence, from conventional and chemical weapons to bombardment, siege, starvation, disappearance, and torture. Some Syrians eventually and inevitably answered with violence, and Syria soon unraveled into civil and proxy war, midwifed by external countries eager to inflict their own ambitions for power or settle scores with their enemies. As if that were not enough, then came along the so-called caliphate for its turn at the one-upmanship in barbarity. Though many of the fighters who traveled to Syria to participate in this dystopian violence were foreign, European and other Western countries bombed Syria to prevent these fighters from carrying out attacks in Europe and beyond.

Not without cause, many Syrians thus refer to theirs as the "stolen" revolution. Whether it was the regime that employed violence to hold on to power or the armed groups wielding violence to wrest and claim that power, Syrian civilians paid the price.

Rejecting this political whirlpool, millions fled the country. Just in 2015, nearly a million risked the Mediterranean Sea to reach countries beyond Syria's immediate neighbors, where it was increasingly clear, even then, that Syrians would be doomed to a life of purgatory. With their sights set on Europe, traveling on flimsy rafts and with fraudulent life jackets, hundreds were swallowed by the waters. For those who made it out of Syria, they found that safety from a war zone also came with displacement, exile, and the indignities of being refugees in places that were not necessarily welcoming.

When on February 6, 2023, the 7.8-magnitude earthquake struck, it was followed almost immediately by a 6.7-magnitude aftershock and, in the coming days, by yet more earthquakes and more aftershocks. Syrians would tell me, as I reported from Turkey in the months after the earthquake, that the deafening sound of the earth itself breaking beneath them and rent asunder from depths below was how they imagined Judgment Day.

By the time Syrians in Turkey experienced this new kind of terror, they were already veterans of many other horrors, and each time, they hadn't believed the last could be superseded. "The only thing we haven't seen," Syrians would tell me, "are dinosaurs and volcanos."

* * *

This is not a collection about *the* earthquake. It's a collection of fiction—short stories, novel excerpts, and plays—that explores the aftershocks that follow a seismic event.

All but one of the pieces in this collection were originally written in Arabic, and all but one were written after 2011, an era in which multiple such events occurred in succession. But even within these works, it becomes clear that there are still so many older, long-ago-sustained fissures, their impact yet ever present, having cleaved lands, borders, peoples, and people. It is not surprising that without any reconciliation, these past quakes, many of which are steeped in human rights violations and injustices, and the scarred terrain they left behind gave rise to what would come for Syria and Syrians in this era. The ongoing and compounded nature of these aftershocks also makes clear that these are not finite events.

The writers in this collection show us that a population's diverse ethnic and religious makeup, which in other contexts could be a strength, has in today's Syria meant multiple potential fault lines. While of course their impact is felt politically, these fault lines are also very personal, shaping or mutating the trajectories of individual lives. And for many of the characters in these stories, what (finally) breaks them or causes the most damage are the personal shocks, which might seem trivial in comparison to the unraveling of an entire country and the fraying of its societal fabric.

A young man, who during his mandatory conscription likely witnesses the unspeakable, is undone instead when the woman he loves marries another. A daughter exiled in Europe begins to realize her father might be guilty of what he is accused of. Families are alive and uninjured but split apart by cracks that run the length of countries, continents, and oceans, their family bonds atrophying in diaspora. When grandparents finally meet their grandchildren, years after the children have said their first words—though in a language they do not share—they are not much more than strangers to each other.

In a war, particularly one that pits neighbor against neighbor, even blood against blood, as happened (is happening) in Syria, the bonds between the requisite actors in any conflict (and crime)—victim, killer, survivor—are often quite intimate. One story refers to this threesome as the "trinity." They are all here in this collection, with their pain, grief, loss, shock, rage, guilt, and self-loathing. So are each one's resentments and accusations against the other. Perhaps because of that intimacy, individuals can, at shifting points, belong to all three groups. As is often the case in real life, the victims in some of these stories go on to victimize others. Likewise, the killers and perpetrators are also victims themselves. Even the survivors are liminal.

For decades before 2011, Syrians understood that to survive under totalitarian rule, where no dissent is tolerated, they'd have to remain silent. That most Syrians abided by this bargain was by no means an endorsement of the regime—people simply went along to get along. Those who didn't not only paid with their own life or liberty but were also gambling with the lives of their families, whom the regime would not hesitate to target for the sins of their relatives. Thus the regime very effectively extracted submission. But by carrying on with life under such terms, as if this were *normal*, the people are not only victims of their rulers but also their collaborators.

In one story, two strangers are seated side by side on a bus traveling from one city to another—a common occurrence anywhere in the world. The subtext of the small talk between them, however, is exile, death, and enforced disappearance. Though such suffering should have stopped the world or at least interrupted every Syrian's life, it is instead as common as the bus ride, a shameful normalization of horror. Similarly, a chasm opens between those for whom there is no going back to any kind of before-the-shock and those who pretend it never happened; they are incomprehensible to each other.

For more than one character in the following pages, there is no relief from these tensions and rifts, even in death. It is notable that the dead are very much present in several stories—and not just as memories. The dead live, including those reduced to incomplete skeletons; they haunt and are haunted by who they were and what they did or suffered. Their delusions follow them to their graves.

An overall picture emerges of how Syrians' experiences of the same events and years are so disconnected that Syrians move through parallel versions of life (or the afterlife) sharing little more than time and space.

Only those who have gone mad, afflicted by an inability to pretend life is normal and having nothing to lose, insist on acknowledgment, on reality. In one story, this is chillingly conveyed by a boy who has taken a position above a bus shelter, taunting passengers waiting for the bus by dangling a noose (for reasons that are revealed in the end) above them, lassoing here and there a head.

When an apparatus of surveillance (like that on which the Syrian regime was built and maintained) is truly effective, the people self-surveil, self-censor, and self-silence. Even if the noose is not physically present, you still feel it around your neck, and your only choice is whether to step off the ledge. Or as the warning goes, "Shh, the walls have ears." Before 2011, the prospect of being informed on was so terrifying that Syrians, even those outside Syria, would drop their voices when talking about the regime, lest they be overheard.

Still today, with the regime intact and undeterred, this fear and these practices persist and have followed Syrians into diaspora. There are many credible reports that the regime is keeping tabs on Syrian refugees in other countries. While the regime's reach is diminished at that distance, it is still very much operative in Syria, which is why any suggestion that Syria is safe (as a precursor to returning the refugees) is preposterous.

As a result, ordinary people have spent decades perfecting small and coded talk. I saw this clearly in Damascus in August 2011 when I attended a group therapy session led by a Syrian Jesuit priest who was also a psychotherapist.

At the time, it had become clear that unlike Tunisia and Egypt, where long-ruling dictators relinquished power with relatively little violence, Syria would be bloody. It already was. Syrians needed to speak, especially to each other, but with the regime quick to clamp down on any activity, while simultaneously insisting nothing was happening (at one point they claimed news networks had faked the footage of protests), people could not talk openly.

In the basement of this church, Syrians of all ages and sects had gathered to discuss their anxiety and fears about what might happen in the country. (In retrospect, those were well-justified concerns.) The therapy method was psycho-drama—in which members act out an imagined scenario. At the session I attended, the participants pretended they were at a conference to discuss their dreams. One man said he'd play the part of the government minder, who would be there if this conference were real.

What unfolded was disturbing; though it was only make-believe, the sense of menace each time the "government man" spoke was palpable. Even in this imagined situation, Syrians were not able to talk directly to each other about what was happening in their country. They were able to begin to talk to each other only by pretending to just be pretending.

This way of speaking with plausible deniability makes its way onto the page here in the works that use allegory or anthropomorphism or invented places, all of which are nonetheless recognizable. Many of the writers use elements of magical realism. We have corpses—casualties of an unspecified war and unspecified sectarianism—revived by letters smuggled in their bodies. Skeletons fall in love, minarets bleed. While the style may extend from the inability to write freely, the insertion of the fantastical into our plane of existence aptly mirrors the absurdity of the last thirteen years.

That said, a non-embellished reality is absurd enough, as seen in the stories that eschew caution. In one work—on the surface, a story taken from the headlines—a Syrian refugee is arrested in Europe for the torture he oversaw while in Syria. But as a cog in a massive system that has enjoyed rampant impunity, any trial promises a kind of justice ridiculous in its inadequacy. In another, a small child born after his father was disappeared cannot grasp that the newly freed man is his parent, having been told his whole short life that his father is the photograph his mother has always shown him.

Across many of the works, there are moments when the reader—and the protagonists, for that matter—is unsure what is real and what is not. In a few, the question is more specific: What are dreams and what is just waking slumber? One offers us a play within a play—which one is the actual one? For some characters, this murky line between the real and imaginary is a kind of dissociative self-preservation; for others it is a genuine uncertainty.

After all, as I write this, it has been six months of Gaza's liquidation—I do not know whether the killing will be done by the time this volume comes out. But from the cruelty and impunity we saw proliferate in Syria to these unending days watching and *witnessing* readily available—more than ever before—accounts of annihilation on platforms where other people post pictures of food, cats, and outfits, our lives still go on. This dissonance surely diminishes our entire humanity. That the sum of our accomplishments as a species has brought us here—what question can be asked other than, if not "what is real?" then "*how* can this be real?"

THE MAN WHO IS NO LONGER A FATHER

by IBRAHIM SAMU'IL
translated by GHADA ALATRASH

HAS IT EVER HAPPENED to you that you suddenly discovered you are not the father of your son? Before you rush to answer, let me clarify that I am not talking about the kind of discovery that takes place in Egyptian movies, where the hero calls out for his young son while on his deathbed, wailing and mourning, and then reveals to him in Shakespearean-tragedy style that he is not his father. Obviously, this is not what I am talking about; I am referring to what happened to Nazir Raheem Al-Omar, who suddenly discovered that he was no longer—after having been—the father of his son.

I say "after having been" because Nazir is indeed the father of his son, Khaled. Khaled is Nazir's son, and his name—up until the writing of this story—is still written in the family registry as "Khaled *bin* Nazir Raheem Al-Omar." Yes, and Mariam Raheem Al-Omar—Nazir's cousin before marriage—is Nazir's wife; she was not married to anyone before him, and he has not married anyone other than her. This is confirmed in his family registration documents, where there is no indication of any wives other than Mariam.

Anyway, I think the situation is simple and straightforward when it comes to the kinship and succession of relations in the family of Mr. Nazir Raheem Al-Omar—well, except for this urgent problem that obstructed the life of the family, and in particular Nazir's, or rather, to be more precise, the relationship between Khaled and his father, Nazir, where the latter came to realize that he is no longer the father of his son after having been so, as I've already told you.

There's no denying that this discovery would not have caused a problem in Nazir's life had it stayed within reasonable boundaries. However, it went way too far; in fact, Nazir has recently reached a truly terrible state of failure that has created a problem that neither he nor his friends nor his relatives would have anticipated. Who would have thought that a man like Nazir could fail to convince his son that he is his father and that Khaled... Oh, I just remembered something—what added to the complexity of the problem is that Khaled also suddenly realized that his father is not his father; I mean that this bald man, the one without a hat on his head, beard on his face, or black sunglasses on his eyes, is not his father!

You might say: *Then the difference of appearance must not have been that big of a deal.* I, like you, initially thought so. But I later learned that Nazir had resorted to thousands of methods and approaches including patience, wittiness, and maneuvering, and after all failed and he'd almost given up, he even grew a beard, wore a hat, and put on sunglasses—but all to no avail, as Khaled continued to look at (and refer to) Nazir as an "uncle"; best-case scenario, while joyfully opening his gifts, Khaled added the word *al-habbab* (the loving), making Nazir "the Uncle *al-habbab*." But to be called baba, as Nazir yearned and burned to hear, was a wish in vain! Imagine that Khaled did not once, even mistakenly, call him baba, as he called the father in the picture hanging on... Oh, that's right! How did I forget to tell you the story of the picture, which happens to be the cause of the problem, or at least a part of it, as it was Mariam who hung the picture on the wall in her husband's absence? For, if I may say so, I believe that Mariam is the reason behind our problem. Anyway, regardless of who was the root of the problem, it's not for me to say, and I'll leave it up to you to decide—but what I will say is that the picture is a very ordinary one. It was a picture like all the others once taken by Nazir while he was wanted and in hiding, disguised with a hat, beard, and black sunglasses. After marrying Mariam, he enlarged it and placed it on top of the wardrobe among a collection of letters, papers, and many other things that belonged to him. Yes, and the picture, as per Mariam, remained there until the night of March 25, 1979, around one o'clock in the morning. On that night, according to Mariam, someone knocked violently and persistently on the door of their home—the sort of knocking that had become common in the country. As Nazir opened the door, six or seven armed individuals descended upon him and raided the room and turned it upside down. Then, as Nazir recounts, they took him away, along with a few confidential documents, newspapers, and books with red covers, leaving Mariam with her swollen belly (Mariam says she was in the ninth month of pregnancy and the eleventh month of marriage), which rose and fell with her rapid breathing. Anyways, long story short, Nazir went with them, leaving behind his wife and personal belongings, including the picture that later played a role in creating the problem we are talking about.

I am sure that that story about what happened to Nazir on that night is not new to you, as you must have surely heard about it from your neighbors or relatives. However, I would like to add a small piece of information here, one that you may be unaware of—you see, Nazir's absence from his home was not just for five minutes, as the chief officer had promised; instead, Nair was absent for much longer—three years to be precise.

And so, as Nazir began to sink into darkness, caught in a web of armed officers, Mariam rushed back into the house after having walked him to the door. As if awakening from what seemed like a nightmare, she climbed on a wooden chair, and from among the stacks of papers, books, and magazines, she reached for Nazir's dusty picture and wiped it with her tightened chest. Holding his picture in her hands felt as if she had pulled him away from them and that he had returned to her. She kissed his beard, hat, and sunglasses, slipped back into the bed they were in just moments before, and she embraced him close to her body. The only thing separating them was a fleshy mass, swollen like a balloon, one that dissolved after about ten days and became the boy who was later named Khaled.

We won't get into Nazir's overdramatization about how he believed that the problem began when Mariam held his picture to her belly on the night of his arrest and that his son was introduced to the picture even before his birth, a picture that had become engraved in his bones, blood, and mind—for in reality, the problem was born after Khaled's birth and then began to grow with him as he grew up in the house.

What confirms this belief is that Mariam, throughout the years of her husband's imprisonment, continued to share Nazir's picture in both big and small moments—while feeding Khaled as an infant, she would place him on the bed, give him a bottle, and bring Nazir's picture a bit closer to him so that he could stare it as he drank his milk; when Khaled cried, she would playfully distract him with the photo and he would eventually forget about his crying. At the age of ten months, she taught him the word *ba... ba* before teaching him how to say *mama*. And when Mariam celebrated his first birthday, the picture was as present as her and Nazir's friends, and it even participated in the eating of the cake! And so it was that as Khaled grew up, the picture also grew with him. The father in the picture would get upset with him when he broke a dish and was happy with him when he finished the food on the plate. He would bid his son farewell at the window before he left for kindergarten and would greet him with toys and candy when he returned in the afternoon. He would sit with Khaled and his mother at the head of the dining table and sleep between them in bed at night. There was not a toy rifle, ball, coloring book, stuffed monkey or elephant owned by Khaled—as Khaled would tell it—that was not bought by his father.

Of course, this was all Mariam's doing, for each time Khaled returned home from kindergarten, he ran to his mother and asked her excitedly, "Mama, what did Baba bring me today?" She would then answer teasingly, "I don't know! Ask him." Before finishing her sentence, the son would run to his father—I mean, to the picture of his father placed on the table—and without waiting for an answer, he would move the picture aside and find a teddy bear, a book, or some pieces of candy. After quickly kissing whatever it was that he had received, he would rush to his friends in the neighborhood to show off his new gift from his father.

So many times, says Mariam, as Khaled gave her a hard time while growing up, she would threaten to tell his father, who was surely going to be upset with him; and so, he would obey and make her swear not to tell him. There were also so many times that Khaled complained about her to his father!

Yes, she often she saw him sneak behind her back and stand in front of the mirror crying and stammering about how his mother did not allow him to play with his friends in the neighborhood, did not buy him ice cream, or did not take him to the swings!

One interesting incident that Mariam narrated, which may help us understand the gravity of the problem, was when she had found Khaled in the neighborhood, scolded him, and brought him back into the house. As he began to cry and shout, "I swear, Mama, it was Baba who allowed me to play," she was shocked and accused him of lying. But he insisted and rushed to the picture as his witness, saying, "Baba, didn't you allow me to play in the neighborhood?" Coincidentally, the picture shook at the movement of Khaled's hand on the table, and so he turned to his mother victoriously saying, "See? He did allow me!"

As such, three years passed after which Nazir was released from prison, but the picture continued to imprison him!

As happens to be the case after a long imprisonment, Nazir embraced Mariam and cried, and she also embraced him for a long time and cried. "But," says Nazir sadly, "as I turned to Khaled and embraced him to my chest, I felt like there was a rock between him and me! I felt his terrified shock—it may have been because he saw me hugging his mother or because he saw his mother crying, or perhaps it was something else. However, I felt like I was pulling a metal spring to my chest! I hugged him with longing while he felt like a rock in my arms."

Nazir tried again and again afterward. He sought the help of Mariam, his friends, and his relatives. He would stand at the window, wave goodbye, and welcome his son with toys and candy. He imitated everything the photo did in his absence, but to no avail! Everyone assured him that time was medicine, but the sickness was getting worse and its symptoms multiplied. Even Mariam saw doubt and accusation in Khaled's eye as he stared at her with a look that sneered silently: "You're a liar, Mama."

I am not able to tell you what has happened since, because I've lost contact with Nazir after his family moved from Damascus to Aleppo. However, I did hear from one of Nazir's acquaintances that Khaled was still naughtily playing in the neighborhood with his friends; and when asked if his father was home, he never said that he wasn't, but would instead rush to the door and knock on it rapidly and forcefully. And even when Nazir was the one to open the door, you would see Khaled push him aside, run inside to the room, jump on a chair, and joyfully announce to his father in the picture, "Baba, your friends are here; your friends are here."

—*March 1987*

THE THINGS THAT HEAVEN CANNOT TELL PEOPLE

by MUSTAFA TAJ ALDEEN ALMOSA
translated by MAISAA TANJOUR *and* ALICE HOLTTUM

WAR HAS MIRACLES THAT minds are unable to comprehend, and anyone who has lived in a city at war is fully aware of this.

It is said that time will reorder the chaos of things, albeit to a modest degree, and this is what people have begun to notice recently, after years of war, as they remember their circumstances in the first year of battle.

When the clashes erupted in our city, utter chaos ensued, but with the passage of time the war began to follow a rhythm. Affairs were gradually arranged between the northern neighborhoods that were controlled by one sect and the southern neighborhoods that were governed by another. The bloody battles therefore ended up confined to the market area in the center of the city as the two sides took turns in displacing, killing, capturing, and exchanging those who belonged to sects other than theirs. The clashes and the exchange of fire even stopped occurring on a daily basis when they agreed to have two ceasefire days per week; one was dedicated to the loathed exchange of the dead and prisoners and the other to the hurried trading of various goods.

Dr. Sulaiman had taken on the task of arranging, recording, and wrapping the corpses in a medical center designated for this purpose after receiving them from the fighters. He would then supervise their delivery in the market area to Dr. Mahmoud, who had undertaken the same task as authorized by the other party. Each of the doctors would then return to his practice with the corpses that belonged to his group. They examined the bodies to find out the nature of the torture that their owners had been subjected to before death. They recorded their findings in a report for the fighters' command and would then work on stitching up the wounds of the corpses, cleaning them, and shrouding them so that they could finally be handed over to their families.

Although the two doctors had studied together at the university, their births into two different sects meant that the war had forced them, like tens of thousands of others, to go to the neighborhoods that suited their respective group.

One day, while they made their exchange among the rubble of the main street in the market, Dr. Sulaiman slipped a note into Dr. Mahmoud's hand. "Read this carefully and consider it with a calm mind," he whispered seriously, winking at him with his left eye.

Dr. Mahmoud quickly took the piece of paper and put it in his pocket, looking around at the volunteers who were helping with the exchange process.

On the way back he read the note several times, and in the following days he thought carefully about its content, scratching his chin uncertainly. He soon came to like the idea that Dr. Sulaiman was proposing.

In the days that separated that meeting from the next, Dr. Mahmoud began to imagine his colleague Dr. Sulaiman entering the room and standing before him. He imagined hearing his voice repeating the words written on that piece of paper: "My dear friend, the war has been going on for years, and now we have an opportunity to improve our situation, yours and mine. How about hiding valuables—jewelry and money— inside the bodies we swap over every week? We profit, and it will also benefit others. If you agree, we can both spread the word that we have contacts among the fighters, then we can deliver some deposits to the other side in exchange for a certain fee. What do you think?"

"I agree." Dr Mahmoud repeated this phrase silently whenever he opened his colleague's note. He then uttered it before him in a low, trembling voice when they met a week later among the ruins of the market.

In the following days, both of the doctors spread the word among their acquaintances in their respective areas that they could deliver valuables to the other side. This was good news and was welcomed by many, because when the people were displaced, most of them had left behind various treasures, which they wanted back, and also because there was a dearth of foreign currency, vital to many on both sides. Others planned to help those who had been their neighbors before the separation, away from the eyes of the fighters of their sect or the militants of the other.

Those who heard the news supposed that each doctor must be in communication and have good relations with the fighters, enabling them to safely deliver the deposits in exchange for material gains, which they would share with the fighters.

And so various people began intermittently to go to the two doctors, passing them valuables and paying them to deliver these to addresses on the other side; they did not know the specific delivery method.

One day Dr. Sulaiman received five corpses from Dr. Mahmoud. "There's foreign money in the body of the blond man and a few pieces of gold inside the big man," the latter whispered into the other's ear. "I've wrapped them up well with the addresses and sewed up the wounds."

When Dr. Sulaiman returned to his practice, he opened up the bodies' deep wounds and took out the deposits before carrying out his usual work of cleaning, archiving, recording, and shrouding the corpses. The next morning he handed the bodies over to their families, and in the evening he delivered the two deposits to the intended addresses.

It was on the evening of the same day that odd things began for Dr. Mahmoud. He had prepared a bowl of lentil soup and was lamenting the distant nights, which he would always remember, when his sleep was not disturbed by strange happenings.

The soup spoon had not quite touched his lips when he heard a series of quick knocks on the door. Dr. Mahmoud returned his spoon to the bowl. Bewildered, he walked over to find out who was there. The sound of shells was rising from afar, little by little, like a black shadow stretching up the wall, slowly elongating.

"There's nothing worse than late-night visitors," Dr. Mahmoud muttered resentfully.

He quickly swallowed his words when he saw through the peephole his elderly aunt who lived nearby. He had not seen her for months, because during the war years she had begun to suffer from some disturbances in her mind.

He opened the door and invited her in, kissing her hand and hugging her warmly. As soon as she had sat down in front of him, she burst out crying bitterly. She choked on her words as she tried to explain, all the while waving around a piece of paper held between her fingers. "Please, my nephew, I heard that you have contacts who can make deliveries to the other side of the city. I wrote a letter to my husband. I haven't seen him for years, since he was forced to take refuge on the other side after all our children were killed. I wrote this letter to him. I miss him. I remembered that we used to write letters to each other when we were students at the university, and in my loneliness I felt the need to write to him again. Please, deliver this letter to him, and in return take my gold bracelet; you can split the money with your people who do the deliveries."

He held her hand to prevent her from taking off her bracelet, turning his face away as he listened to her continuing sobs. He sighed and took the letter from her. He nodded and promised to deliver it to her husband on the other side, patting her shoulder tenderly. He helped her to get up and walked her slowly to the door.

When he returned to the dinner table he had lost interest in the soup. He opened his aunt's letter and read it, exhaling and sighing every few words, agonizing for his aunt and her husband. The words of her letter were a clear example of her mental turmoil.

"There's some cash wrapped up with an address in the woman's corpse, and there's a letter inside the young man with the long hair. I've wrapped it up together with the delivery address. Don't be surprised: it's from my aunt; she begged me to deliver it to her husband who lives in your part of town. Please, don't be shocked. Crazy things happen in wars. The war itself is a crazy thing. My aunt's condition is miserable and heart-wrenching. She's not right—her children were all killed and her husband was displaced. Let's make her wish come true. Her husband's house isn't far from your practice. Please do give the letter to him."

Dr. Sulaiman felt very flustered upon hearing these words as some of the volunteers behind them arranged the corpses on stretchers. On a previous night, as he had closely watched the war from his balcony, he became convinced that it was indeed crazy, but he had never imagined that this insanity would make corpses into postmen, carrying messages between the war zones in this disaster-stricken city. Even the imagination could never come up with such madness. The body was now a post carrier, and the letter was inside! Unlike imagination, the grotesqueries of war seemed to have no limits.

Both doctors were speechless. The words vanished from their lips as, with trembling hands, they joined the rest of the volunteers in zipping the black plastic bags over the blood-soaked corpses so that they could be taken back to their respective medical centers.

Nor would the grotesqueness end here. It would now imbibe the war as its wine and wobble, horribly drunk, between the fates of two doctors, taking the form of a dark series of unbelievable events, a series that only they among the inhabitants of the city would be able to see.

The volunteers helped Dr. Sulaiman transport the corpses back to his office and get them inside. Then they went home. The doctor opened the woman's corpse to take out the coins; they were tightly wrapped with the address of their owner inside a deep wound. He moved to the body of the long-haired young man, intending to open his wound to extract the letter his colleague's crazy old aunt had written.

He was initially confused; there was something odd about the man's body. It was as though a slow, faint pulse, like the light of a dying candle, was still present inside it. He examined the body hastily to discover, his breath racing in his chest, that the young man was still alive. Dr. Sulaiman immediately used the defibrillator on him, then connected tubes and devices to various parts of his emaciated body. After hours of painstaking work tending to the wounds, Dr. Sulaiman was sure that the young man would regain consciousness in the morning.

Out on his balcony Dr. Sulaiman lit a cigarette and took a deep drag. He then exhaled for a long time. He was in shock. He did not understand. Had the fighters on the other side and his colleague Dr. Mahmoud not noticed that this young man was not, in fact, dead? Or had he really died and come back again? The war was insane; it was the perfect time for bizarre things to happen.

He went back to check on the young man and noticed an improvement in his pulse and breathing. He contemplated his chest. In the depths of that chest was a letter written by a mad old woman. Dr. Sulaiman could not get it out; he would not. He must protect the life of this young man.

Dr. Sulaiman did not sleep well that night; his slumber was disturbed by nightmares. In the morning, he handed the corpses over to their relatives, then called the young man's family. A few hours after they had arrived, the man began to regain some consciousness. None of them could understand why the fighters would hand over an injured person without a ransom or anything else in return. They guessed that fate was on their side and thanked God several times. After two days, the man's health had improved enough for his family to take him home. Dr. Sulaiman waved goodbye. At the door of his practice, he imagined it was the letter that stood in front of him. Then it started drifting away, and he could not deliver it to its addressee, so he waved until the letter disappeared into the distance.

The next day, the old husband of Dr. Mahmoud's aunt came to Dr. Sulaiman. The bombing was severe. He introduced himself with tearful eyes. He told the doctor in a warm voice heavy with longing that he had heard from acquaintances about his ability to deliver goods and begged him in a voice wearied from the horrors of war to take a letter to the other side. His wife, whom he had not seen for years, lived there. He offered Dr. Sulaiman a modest sum of money. The doctor refused the money and took the letter from the old man's pale hands. His heart breaking for him, he promised to deliver it. He did not tell him about his wife's letter, which was buried in a young man's body and would remain there forever. He kept this secret interred deep in his heart.

After the old man had left, Dr Sulaiman inserted the letter into a wound on one of the corpses, then sewed it up. The next morning, among the ruins of the market, he took Dr. Mahmoud aside. He told him quickly about the corpse of the young man with the long hair that had come back to life in such a mind-blowing way. Dr. Sulaiman asked his colleague whether the young man had definitely been deceased and watched as dark colors crept in turn with the trembling words over the features of Dr. Mahmoud. The latter swore that the young man had certainly been dead a few days ago. They understood from each other that he had indeed come back to life in an incredible way and that the letter was still inside him without his knowledge. Dr. Sulaiman then told his colleague that the circle of strange coincidences had been completed yesterday when an old man, his aunt's husband, had visited him, also with a letter, and begged him to deliver it to the other side of the city, and it was now hidden in the body of the brown-haired young woman who lay among the corpses.

Dr. Mahmoud pitched forward, almost passing out; Dr. Sulaiman grabbed him before he fell to the ground. Dr. Mahmoud felt suffocated, dizzy from the horror of these coincidences so unendurable to the human mind. He did not know how he got to his medical center with the corpses. Everything felt surreal, as though he were in another world, a deranged world.

Dr. Mahmoud had stopped being able to hear anything—the words of Dr. Sulaiman when he had bid him farewell or those of the volunteers in the car or their talk at the practice as they brought in the shrouded corpses to lay them on the beds before departing. He was in a daze. He had not heard any words uttered during the past few hours; everyone's lips moved in front of him, but he no longer heard or understood anything.

Once alone, he hurried to the bodies and removed their covers, one by one, making sure that they were dead. He reached the corpse of the young woman whose wound had been stitched up by Dr. Sulaiman after he had stuffed the letter inside it. He examined the body doubtfully and his heart sank when he saw that the young woman was still alive, though the flame of life in her body was on the verge of going out. He hurried to his medical instruments and proceeded to treat her for several hours until he was sure that her condition was stable. The letter of his aunt's husband remained inside her body. He was able to save the young woman, but he could not save the letter. A few days later a dark-haired young woman left the medical center, leaning on her family members, walking away from Dr. Mahmoud. There was a letter inside her that she did not know about.

In the following weeks, this bizarre occurrence was repeated several more times, and the doctors could find no scientific explanation for it. They could attribute it, as they stood in the midst of their clouds of cigarette smoke, only to the madness of war.

One day, while exchanging the corpses, the pair raised their heads and looked up to the sky. They felt as if only the sky knew their secret, the secret of the letters entombed in the bodies; the letters that would never reach their addressees. Instead, there were corpses coming back to life, the same corpses in which those letters were buried. What utter insanity was this? No one would believe it if they said anything.

Here, in a bleak room a disturbed old woman kept writing letters to her husband in the north of the city, undaunted by his lack of response.

At the same time, over there, a weary old man sat in his modest room writing letters to his wife in the south of the city, undismayed by her lack of reply.

As for those whose bodies had come back to life after a short departure, they returned to their normal lives, none of them realizing that there was a letter inside them, hidden under a large carefully stitched wound. Instead of a grave embracing their bodies, their bodies had become graves to those wretched letters.

As time passed, the number of people returning to life thanks to the letters increased, as the doctors confirmed to each other during their gloomy meetings at the market.

Following hours of exhausting work, Dr. Sulaiman was sure that the condition of this particular wounded man was stable. He was breathing well now, and his heartbeat was almost normal. A few hours ago, he had been a lifeless corpse, like all the others the doctor had received today. He had a deep wound inside of which Dr Mahmoud had deposited a letter. After the exchange, he discovered, as usual, that life had tremulously returned to the dead body. His work had saved the man but, as always, lost the letter.

The exhausted doctor walked away from the wounded man and went out to his balcony. He looked at the people as they moved along the street. They were walking confidently. Today was one of the twice-weekly truce days. He lit a cigarette and took a deep drag as the sun set slowly in the west, coloring the sky with a bloody orange tinge.

It was a quiet evening. Dr. Sulaiman raised his head to blow his cigarette smoke high. His soul was burdened by the secrets that he could never have conceived of encountering. They were like a film based on an outlandish story, a film written and directed by an ominous fate.

He looked at the sky for a long time. He was sure that it was watching all the things that were happening on earth beneath it, but it would never tell the people these stories of their lives or else they would inevitably lose their minds.

"They wouldn't believe me if I told them about the letters, about the bodies coming back to life," he said to himself, turning his eyes away from the bloody sunset. "The things that heaven can't tell people, I can't either."

Dr. Sulaiman began humming one of his favorite songs in a low voice. He had not sung the words of this song since the war started. He had forgotten it, but he remembered it now.

He watched people from his balcony with sad eyes as he sang wearily. He thought about how at this exact moment those people in the street had no idea that some of them had miraculously come back to life. The once-dead now lived with us under the same sky, but neither the resurrected nor the rest of the people knew that inside their war wounds there were letters.

an excerpt from the novel
The Russian Quarter

THE GIRAFFE
AND NONNA

by KHALIL ALREZ

translated by MARGARET LITVIN

I.

ONE DAY NONNA DISCOVERED scallions, as though seeing them for the first time, and bought a bundle.

She was new to Damascus and not yet used to eating fresh scallions, not even with bread and yogurt. But she suddenly knew why she had bought the bundle on the day she met me, for the first time, on the front steps of the Russian Cultural Center downtown in the old capital Damascus.

I was balancing a bale of old newspapers that I had bought by the kilo from the center's library to use in the zoo's wall newspaper. Nonna, holding the bundle of scallions with evident pride, was suddenly struck by the sight of me, and started to scrutinize me as though conjuring me up from distant places and remembered events. Then she made as if to jump forward and embrace me, newspapers and all, but hesitated at the last moment and stayed where she was. However, red-faced now and with pink lips trembling, she held out the bunch of scallions, as though presenting a bouquet. And at that moment I, too, was ready to embrace her, newspapers notwithstanding: not because I had ever seen her before, as both of us might at that moment have believed, but because, at that anguished time I was living through, I had managed to attract the attention of a woman like her.

"Remember me? I'm Nonna!" she asked warmly, and I pressed the tottering bale of papers to my chest with one hand while with the other I received the bundle of scallions and her elevated feelings, as though accepting a bouquet of roses. "I remember you! Wait for me here," she added, and ran up the stairs, disappearing into the Russian Cultural Center.

In fact I almost didn't want to remember her. The stack of newspapers had grown lighter, the appetizing stalks of scallion were near my face, and the passersby seemed less irritable and more harmonious; I didn't need there to be, or not to be, an old story linking me to Nonna and secretly foreshadowing our delightful meeting a few minutes ago. I needed no additional interpretations, reasons, or causes to explain her enthusiasm toward me or justify why I was happily standing on the sidewalk in front of the Russian Cultural Center on May 29th Street holding my bale of newspapers and her scallion bouquet. All I cared about at that moment was that I was waiting for a beautiful woman whom I needed with all my might.

Of course, even when she kept me waiting, it did not occur to me to disbelieve either my feelings or my senses. I stood still in my spot, not feeling the time pass, thinking not of her absence but of her. Then I noticed an old blind man following his cane; he hesitated for a moment when he crossed me on the sidewalk, then moved two or three steps away and stood beside a young pine tree. Then he smiled fondly, as though he had just run into a friend in the darkness, the stick confirming his presence with graceful movements through the void in front of him. I didn't want to disturb his joy at whatever he saw. I tried as best I could to let him know that I was not present beside him, and that no one but him saw or expected his dear friend in the total darkness around him; I looked at the sky, distracted by its pure blue. Then the long stick surprised me with a light touch on my knee, as though by coincidence, and I turned to him.

His smile was widening as he gazed from behind his heavy, hooded eyelids toward the entrance of the Russian Cultural Center, where Nonna suddenly appeared at the door. Now she wore a short sleeveless golden-yellow dress that showed the whiteness of her bare arms and legs; a red handbag dangled from her arm. As she quickly and lightly ran down the steps she seemed to me so attractive that I could not recall what she had been wearing before. She stood in front of me almost panting, her parted pink lips and happy eyes awaiting our first steps together in the old capital Damascus.

I looked at the blind man; he was still beaming, most likely because of Nonna and me. Then I imagined that his dear friend whom we couldn't see, the one perhaps still standing in front of him in his velvet darkness beside the pine tree, was blessing us with the same big grin. I bid them both farewell with a gentle nod, then raised my hand to hail a taxi to take Nonna and me to the zoo in the Russian Quarter.

II.

Nonna and her scallions were two important life events for the giraffe.

My table had never lacked scallions, especially in the spring—either in the vegetable bowl with the green pepper, radishes, and pea sprouts next to my bowl of yogurt and rice; or in with the peas and carrots stewed in tomato juice; or minced with parsley and fried onions into patties of bulgur or lentil *tshika*; or perhaps on their own, dropped with a sprinkling of salt into a hot pita. The giraffe had followed along with her usual intense curiosity as I ate my supper in front of her on the roof, enveloped in an aroma of scallions that no one else in the zoo seemed to feel, expect, or sense. I had never noticed how hungrily the giraffe would inhale my breath whenever I patted her face and ruffled her mane after supper. I would put the wicker chair at the edge of the roof and sit across from her, just like someone who had eaten no supper at all. Before Nonna came I could draw no connection, not even the slimmest, between the giraffe's enthusiastic sniffing and the scent of scallions I radiated—in fact, it had pleased me to be the sole target of her warm feelings. Whereas Nonna figured out the giraffe's love of scallions right away, from their first meeting.

She had preceded me up the stairs to my room on the zoo roof, because I had first detoured to Victor Ivanitch's office to drop off the bale of newspapers. The length of the stairway to the roof allowed me to catch up with her at the very top, catching a first glimpse of her back in the golden-yellow dress with blond locks overflowing onto her shoulders.

As soon as she saw the giraffe's head facing her from the edge of the opposite roof, she gasped with surprise. She reached out a hand for the bouquet of scallions, took it from me without thought or hesitation, and approached the giraffe as one approaches a huge beloved aunt. Then, stalk by stalk, in leisurely fashion, she began feeding her the whole green bundle.

I had often noticed how distractedly the giraffe chewed stalks of grass or leaves, her eyes clouded over with one steady endless thought. Sometimes I would bring a clump of her grass up to the roof so that we could have supper tête-à-tête, but even then her one long and probably boring thought distracted her during the whole meal. Now, with the first scallion she took from Nonna's hand, I waited for the same old familiar thought to possess her mind. But this time she kept chewing the scallion and smacking her lips for a long time, her eyes shining as though with feelings and images that were new, sweeter and more delicious. Then she seemed to be so enchanted by her fresh and fragrant treat that she started murmuring to us, and perhaps to herself, in soft and firm tones that flowed from her flattened nostrils.

As she swallowed her first scallion and began on the second with the same lip-smacking care, I watched the old dull thought vanish from her eyes and considered: Victor Ivanitch would certainly refuse to change her diet of faded grass and withered leaves. No, he would never agree to feed her scallions, no matter how much he respected her as the hugest being not only in the Russian Quarter but in the whole old city of Damascus. As the general director of the zoo and editor of its wall newspaper, he always looked at every little coin with eyes for the black day that might never come but might come at any moment. Our allocation from the Russian Quarter municipal budget barely covered our minimum expenses. As for Borya, the zoo couldn't rely on his financial assistance for any kind of planning; his help simply didn't come regularly enough, even if it was true that he largely kept the zoo carnivores fed with his haul of game during hunting season. "But he leaves their jaws hanging open for the whole rest of the year, so what am I supposed to do with that?" Victor Ivanitch complained one day in the wall newspaper's opening editorial, even though, in fact, our only carnivores were a hyena, a grumpy and unhungry fox, the elderly wolf couple, and three black eagles that usually made do with the proceeds of the zoo's rat traps.

In short, it was no use bringing up the matter of scallions for the giraffe with Victor Ivanitch. And notwithstanding her faith in and affection for the giraffe, many reasons made it difficult, not to say impossible, for Nonna to provide twenty-five kilograms of scallions per day at her own personal expense. However, after a very brief back-and-forth with me she determined to continue to offer her scallions every day as a fresh dessert after her long and withered main meal. That very day she began setting aside one bunch for her every evening.

But Nonna's friendship with the giraffe went beyond scallions.

Of course, it did not intrude on the giraffe's warm mutual relationship with the other zoo animals. From the moment she appeared among us, no one thought she was competing with anyone for the giraffe's affection or trying to replace anyone in the dear little favors they wanted to do for the giraffe. Instead, from her first days at the zoo she began to explore, as no one else had ever done, some shadowy unvisited corners of the giraffe's life. For instance, one night she informed me that the giraffe sometimes sang very quietly in the evening stillness, her hoarse voice seeping out from the depths of her long throat. I naturally got caught up in Nonna's discoveries, since these details of the giraffe had escaped me, and together we leaned in close to hear her quiet singing, pressing our ears to her neck with passionate attention. We preferred to believe that her deep, distant heart-rending song expressed belonging, not forlornness.

Then one day Nonna discovered that the giraffe didn't drink water daily but made do with one drink every two or three days and that, moreover, she didn't enjoy getting wet without warning. Nonna made sure to advise everyone to pay attention to the water in her trough and keep it fresh, and to take care not to splash her, even in jest.

At around the same time Nonna also noticed the giraffe's woefully inadequate contingent of birds relative to the large number of ticks and insects hiding in the vast spotted skin. She imagined these easily and made me imagine them too. Nonna thought (and I immediately did too) that the giraffe could not control what the birds did when they left their nests looking for food, and neither could we—we couldn't force them to comb the giraffe's whole hide with their avid beaks every morning. Naturally we also couldn't leave the giraffe's hide as a grazing ground for its many likely insects, so Nonna recalled the clothes brush kept by her father Denis Petrovich in the room he rented at the Russian Cultural Center, and I recalled the iron ladder in the zoo's storage closet. Denis Petrovich didn't mind, Nonna said, but went to the closet and showed her another brand-new iron brush that he had brought from Moscow two years earlier and would now finally have occasion to use.

After that, whenever she felt the giraffe needed relief from her overabundant insects, Nonna would climb to the top rung of the ladder while I steadied it from below and held a pail of water; I would take the brush from her hand, stick it in the pail, swish it around to rinse off the remaining imaginary insects, then dry it on a clean old towel hung over my shoulder before handing it back to her.

"The birds will still find bugs to eat," Nonna would say. "Birds keep hopping around searching for bugs until they find them, and if they don't find them right away they'll keep trying and won't despair, because birds don't know what despair is. At such moments they're part of the giraffe's being, just like her tail or her pile of dry branches. Like Ivanova, who sweeps her droppings every morning, or like me at the top of the ladder, or like you next to the water pail. My arm doesn't reach all the way across the giraffe's back in any case. Even with the ladder I can't get to the bird food up there. And the giraffe herself unconsciously prevents it. She doesn't usually need to think about the details of her life or ours, or analyze how she eats, walks, wakes up, or sees you or me. I mean, she doesn't care exactly what we expect from her—she just senses us as the many creatures who live inside her personal life, and she acts on that basis. That's why the birds will always find bugs to eat in her vast hide, no matter how long their search or how many bugs I pick off." Nonna kept talking, sounding like the giraffe's chief confidante and permanent spokeswoman for her thoughts and feelings, while I watched her diligent hand wield Denis Petrovich's clothes brush fondly and knowledgeably across a tiny area of the giraffe's gargantuan body.

Then came the day when Nonna discovered the giraffe didn't yawn.

"We yawn sometimes, and so do the elderly wolves, the hyena, the foxes, and everyone else at the zoo—as well as the jungle tigers, lions, and leopards we've seen in cartoons and nature shows since childhood, don't you remember?" Nonna asked me. That evening she asked me to keep watch overnight to know whether the giraffe yawned before going to sleep, at least.

"If she yawns while I'm asleep, wake me up right away!" Nonna said, then suddenly walked to the bedroom, going to bed before me for the first time.

I didn't even realize how long it had been since I had been alone with the giraffe. But as soon as I saw myself standing alone on the roof opposite her, I felt my yearning for her, hot and unexpected, as though we hadn't just spent the whole evening together. I didn't like to think that this yearning expressed my desire to repossess the special connection to the giraffe that I had enjoyed before Nonna's arrival but had yielded to her day by day. I was annoyed, in fact, to be blaming my sweet overwhelming weakness toward Nonna for the desolate space that had somehow, in Nonna's strong presence, appeared between the giraffe and me. I won't give in to these delusions so easily, I told myself. I have felt, and will continue to feel, precisely the same sweet overwhelming weakness toward the giraffe as well. Now I approached her, full of dread that she might welcome me less warmly than I expected and hoped.

I sat in front of her on my wicker chair at the edge of the roof, as though the desolate space between us was a miscalculation on my part, nothing more, which I could now try to resolve without meaning in any way (for how could I?) to detract from Nonna's image in the giraffe's mind or, of course, my own. Perhaps by yielding (as I now preferred to call it) to Nonna some of my closeness with the giraffe, I had simply helped each of the three of us to gradually discover how much we needed the other two. True, Nonna's lively presence and rich imagination had filled many previously unnoticed gaps in my understanding of the giraffe's senses, attachments, and concerns. But thanks to Nonna I, too, had become more attentive to these things, which had escaped me before she came to live with me in the zoo.

I stepped closer to the giraffe. I reached out one hand to her mane in greeting and buried the other in the warm spot between her neck and her jaw, scratching there; she bent down her enormous head until it rested on my shoulder. I pressed my cheek to her giant fuzzy wrinkled cheek and closed my eyes, waiting for her to calm my troubled emotions; she didn't keep me waiting long. Right away I felt a distant throat-rumble coming toward me, one of those deep, satisfied rumbles that sometimes rose from her depths when she munched a scallion. I was ready to take this as a sufficient sign of my place in her life, undiminished from the pre-Nonna days. But she immediately pressed her head on my back, gently and with evident affection, as though to allow me to embrace her whole warm, pulsing neck in my arms. I did this with all my strength, as though seizing a singular opportunity to satisfy a desire I had felt for years. And when I moved my head away from her a little, my fingers touching the enormous features of her face, I saw that she was, as I had expected and loved and wanted, gazing at me from the depths of her wide black eyes and open ears, listening to me with the sincere attention that I had always enjoyed. As though she were once more tirelessly searching within me for the trace of her lost calf and for the rustle of her bygone trees, the whisper of her ancient shadows, and the clamor of loving voices that she had lost deep in her past and in the pasts of her grandmother giraffes in her distant, obscure, vanished homeland.

Then I suddenly remembered about her not yawning. I realized that she would not be able to sleep as long as I sat across from her. I rose from the wicker chair and walked to the other edge of the roof, the side overlooking the street. I stood in a corner that allowed me to keep a furtive watch for any yawns while appearing to be busy with something else entirely. In truth I had no reason to be anxious about her; it had never made a difference to me, from one morning to another, until Nonna had noticed that she refrained from yawning. And even if she didn't yawn, surely she was not the only creature on earth like that. In all my life I had never seen a single sparrow yawn, and not our three black eagles at the zoo, and, as far as I knew, fish and jellyfish and squid never yawned underwater, and surely no ant or bee ever found time to yawn during its wearisome busy day. Nonetheless I wanted to respect Nonna's judgment and her sharp eye. More precisely, I wanted her sweet worry for the giraffe to inhabit me too. So without letting the giraffe out of my sight, I now tried, as much as possible, to freeze in place with my eyes fixed on the silhouette of a woman sitting on a distant balcony across the street—it looked like she had sat there since early evening waiting for a dear absent person, but after a long time on the balcony she seemed to despair of his returning tonight, so she stood up, disappointed, and vanished into the dark flat. Then the pedestrians in the street grew less frequent, and the late-night noise coming from the nearby entertainment district grew hushed, and the sky began to lighten while the giraffe stood in her place not sleeping and not yawning. She kept me up until Nonna woke to Raisa Petrovna's arrival on our rooftop in the morning. She didn't ask me about the giraffe, for she knew I would certainly have woken her up for any yawns, but she was surprised to find her still standing in the same place after a whole night. "Didn't she sleep?" she asked.

"The giraffe rarely sleeps. And if she does it's mostly in short snatches, twenty minutes at most, and mostly standing up, of course," Victor Ivanitch answered her for me from the neighboring roof, where he was watching, moved and amazed, while Raisa Petrovna went about her favorite morning work cleaning the giraffe's face. Then he added, "Maybe it's the fear of snakes that prevents deep sleep. Even though this giraffe of ours was born in a circus tent."

Nonna looked at me as if perceiving the lion that lurked, even now, in the ancient inherited forest of the giraffe's mind. She turned to the giraffe lost in thought, as if more deeply overwhelmed by her fear of lions than anyone else. Raisa Petrovna had stepped away, fully satisfied with her caring, diligent work. Nonna walked up to the giraffe and slowly placed a hand on her bumpy forehead as though to muffle the pure sylvan roar probably ringing in her head even now. It was clear, to me at least, that Nonna had absorbed the idea of this supposed long-ago lion; from this morning forth she would keep it next to the scallions, the ticks and birds, the ladder and Denis Petrovich's iron brush and the water pail, the veterinarian Bashir Ghandoureh, Ivanova, Raisa Petrovna, and many more of the giraffe's concerns in her life with us all, along with Victor Ivanitch's jottings about her in the little notebook that he kept and sometimes allowed us to read, where he noted the habits of his charges—objects and living beings, animal and human alike—in the Russian Quarter zoo.

AND THE FAMILY
DEVOURED ITS MEN

by DIMA WANNOUS
translated by ELISABETH JAQUETTE

WE CALLED AUNT MARIANNE, waking her from a nap, and told her we'd spent the evening talking behind her back. "Oh, damn you," she said, uttering her usual catchphrase with that endearing tone. Her voice, coming to us from her home in Damascus, had regained its quietude. The question is always about whether we are keeping in touch with each other. Whenever I call from Beirut, she rushes to interrogate me: "Mama, have you spoken to Ninar? How is she? Tell me she's doing okay... and what about Shaghaf?" Her question about Ninar always makes me laugh. She asks as if months have passed without them having spoken. All of Ninar's reassurances aren't enough; they are as incomplete as my aunt's smile, which is never full unless each one of us has reassured her. I don't know whether her smile is ever full, or whether she prefers Ninar over Shaghaf. Sometimes a mother loves one of her children more than the other. Then we phoned Ninar, who doesn't call Shaghaf by name anymore: she calls her "sister." As if disease strips us of even our names, leaving only the way we are related. I looked at Shaghaf, who has become just a handful of bones covered by a thin layer of skin. She was wearing my loose turquoise skirt and my sky-blue blouse. But even the intense blue wasn't enough to hide the pallor of her skin; instead, it emphasized the dark rings around her clear eyes, making her illness all the more apparent. Lashes no longer shade her eyes, they have all fallen out, leaving too much space for her eyes. We decided to go home and climbed the long staircase, leaning on each other for support. She leaned her weak, slender body on me, and on her shadow, I leaned my weary spirit, my anxiety, and my fear. Fear that the day was near. The day I would be obliged to feel more than I could bear. That moment—the moment we were climbing the stairs—belonged to a dismal place overlooking the edge of emotion. We reached the top of the stairs out of breath. Shaghaf, in her skinny, weary body, was trying to catch her breath, while my soul was calling for help, trying to regain its balance. Going back in time had exhausted me. Or not going back, so much as Shaghaf's need to recover that hidden piece of memory. To reveal what she had not revealed before. To seek shelter from the future by retreating to the past. As if discussing the past in detail would lead us back to it! She wanted to go back in time. I didn't ask whether that would change anything. A silly question. If we had been given the chance to go back in time, we would certainly have changed things; we might even have changed everything. We stood in the wide garage, waiting for a taxi that would take us back to my mother. She took a cigarette from her brown leather purse and I lit it for her, using my palms to cup the lighter. She looked into my eyes and smiled. "I love you."

On my way to Shaghaf's new house for the first time, we drove on that high stretch of road that terrified me when I was small. On our descent, the driver didn't turn left onto the road that leads to Aunt Marianne's house and Shaghaf's old house, we continued straight, down to a two-way street, driving incredibly slowly for fear of crashing. Lush cypress trees arched over us from the right side of the road. The driver turned right, and his car's old engine stuttered and growled at the next steep ascent. My heart didn't growl with it, as it had in the past. We turned down narrow alleys barely big enough for the car, turning right then left then right, until we reached an impasse. I got out of the car and gazed at the doors of the old houses jumbled together. I saw the blue iron door that Shaghaf had told me about. I knocked. I could hear her footsteps drawing closer and imagined her walking toward the door: her short frame, clothed in a short-sleeved loose sweater that just covered her bottom, revealing her harmonious legs. Her right fingers restlessly fondling a strand of her short hair. When she opened the door, she greeted me exactly as I had imagined. She closed it slowly and walked in front of me, leading me to her room. We crossed the small courtyard to one of five doors leading off the circular space. A very small room, with a bed, a couch, and a low table, on which sat an ashtray choked with cigarette butts and a coffeepot where dregs crusted the inside and rim. I sat on the couch while Shaghaf went to the kitchen shared by all five rooms to make coffee. Before stepping out, she asked whether I had let my tongue slip: whether my mother or hers had learned her address. I shook my head. Shaghaf had left her husband's house, where we used to gather nearly every Friday, and rented this room. I was the person closest to her during this time. We weren't connected by shared memories, as she was with my mother, her mother, Ninar, and Yasmina. At the same time, we belonged to the same memory. At the time, I knew no more about her than she wanted me to. I hadn't been witness to her forty years, and I'd never been one to judge others. I listened to her for hours and empathized with her story. She needed empathy, even if out of place. Aunt Marianne, her mother, wasn't empathetic. No, Marianne was dissatisfied with everything that happened, as if the "whole family" had slipped through her fingers, and she was no longer in control. My mother wasn't pleased either. Exhaustingly idealistic. As far as my mother was concerned, there was only right and wrong, and aside from that, only heavy feelings of guilt. Ninar wasn't pleased either. She didn't admit that any of us might slip into depression at any time; she thought our feelings of emptiness, powerlessness, and failure had dragged us into an indulgent state. Until, after many years, she fell into it too. Meanwhile, I made Shaghaf feel content with everything she was experiencing and doing. I listened to her without a glimmer of reproach or blame. To Shaghaf, I was no more than a camera—like the camera I recently bought myself, to gaze with me at my mother and listen to her stories, silence, and wandering thoughts. We need lots of energy to reach the point where we can listen to silence. That's what Shaghaf needed back then. She needed me to listen to her silence, as well as her words and confessions, equally attentively. Humans tend to fear silence. They fill it with words and chatter. They can't bear it. They're only quiet when they plunge into sleep, or death. Shaghaf hadn't truly tasted life until six years prior. Constantly complaining, she was. She got sick quite easily: if a migraine receded, irritable bowel syndrome would take its place, and agonizing pain would begin anew. If the medicine Shaghaf swallowed like bonbons got rid of that pain, then her intestinal ulcers would start to scream. And even if she withstood it all, she couldn't escape the drowsiness and fatigue. I was fifteen when Mother first sent me to Shaghaf's house. Her husband was busy directing a new television series; he was gone from the house most hours of the day, and sometimes into the night. Meanwhile Shaghaf was "sick" and needed care. I lived in their house for several months over the summer holiday. We rarely saw each other. I would find her in the kitchen with a cigarette and the coffeepot at half past six in the morning. She would make me a delicious breakfast and smile while watching me devour it with gusto. Then she would disappear into her room all day, waking again at six or seven in the evening to sit with me for a while, then returning to her room. My aunt was displeased, as was my mother, Ninar of course, and Yasmina. Each had her own evidence and rationale for why Shaghaf was only claiming to be ill, asking for it, inventing it out of thin air, or perhaps it was simply an expression of emptiness and failure. I was convinced that she was ill. And maybe it comforted her that I acknowledged her illness. Sometimes she would call to me, in a voice whose coquettishness no illness or disease could diminish, and ask me to give her a capsule of Lexotanil. I had promised my mother and Aunt Marianne that I wouldn't give her sedatives and that I'd try to steal any I found in her bedside drawer. But I gave them to her, because I knew how desperately she needed them. Also, because I was afraid I would lose her trust in me, and that she would stop telling me her thoughts and feelings. Even now, I don't know why I needed her to reveal such an exhausting number of complicated stories and tiresome, jumbled memories. One time when she was sleeping I opened all the sedative capsules. One after another, I emptied them of the soft white powder they held and closed them up again. After that, I became more generous. She'd ask for two pills

and I'd give her three or four. And she would sleep! The pills
didn't become irrelevant. In essence, Shaghaf didn't need the
pills so much as she needed me to give them to her, one after
another, like bonbons, without reproach or blame.

Weeks, then months, then years went by. At a certain
point, her workplace couldn't keep extending the sick leave
she requested on mornings of bad migraines. She was let go
and forced to take her few belongings back to Aunt Marianne's
house. She couldn't manage to pay rent anymore, not even
that secret little room. She returned to a place she didn't want
to go. How, I wondered, could a woman in her forties own so
few belongings and knickknacks? She didn't create memories,
unlike my mother, who had created them unhurriedly. Shaghaf
had no need for that. Yes, she made a conscious decision not
to carve out memories in the places she lived. Perhaps doing
so would have required a perseverance that Shaghaf never
had. A degree of energy and independence. She had married
at eighteen to relieve herself of responsibility. She wasn't able
to carry her body and soul by herself. She married in order to
have someone who would make her coffee in the mornings,
someone on whose shoulder she could lean her head so full of
scattered thoughts. Their marriage lasted only three or four
years. During that time, she gave birth to a daughter, who was
only a year younger than me. Then she left him in Moscow,
where they had been studying, and returned to a place she
didn't want to go: my aunt Marianne's house. For Shaghaf,
that house was a stopping point between one stage and the

next. Between one life and another. She had gone through decades of her life borrowing lives that did not belong to her. A worker sometimes, a victim at others. A housewife, a wife, a lover. A rebel-against-everything, even against the air she breathed. Or someone mentally disturbed, whose every suicide attempt fails. (After her most recent attempt, Aunt Marianne told her with a tone that balanced gravity with jest: "Give us a break and get it right already.") A society lady or a young flirt who could spark jealousy in a room full of other women. Our "family diva" excelled at every persona she borrowed. She embodied them to the last moment, and gave them so much life they seemed more than borrowed. Then she would shift between one life and the next, without giving us enough time to absorb the switch. We would fall asleep and wake up to a different Shaghaf. A single night was sufficient for her to move her small body from one life into another. She didn't borrow these lives to live them, contend with them, and probe their folds, but to talk about them and possess a story by which to defend her fragile, anxious existence. One time she entered her office at the private oil company carrying adhesive and printed stack of papers with explicit insults toward the boss. She began hanging the papers along the corridors and hallways, in staff offices, and his office too. Then she relished in telling the tale. She recounted the reactions of her colleagues, particularly her boss. Then she was surprised that he gave her a warning! "Of course he would give me a warning," she added. "Baathist upbringing..." Shaghaf didn't commit such a foolish act, of unknown consequences, for the sake of the act itself. She did it for the story! She wrote stories in her head and then acted them out so she could tell them to us, indifferent to the looks from my aunt Marianne, whose expression betrayed her anger amid painful silence. She raised her left eyebrow, half closing her eyes, pursed her lips to the left, and shook her head, announcing her despair and inability to control her daughter. Shaghaf attempted suicide in order to tell us what went through her head in the moment before she took a whole bottle of sedatives. Another time she made her way to the polling station early in the morning—Shaghaf, who couldn't bear to leave the house early!—to look the official in the eye and vote "No" against Bashar al-Assad. They detained her. My mother turned to a psychiatrist friend, and he gave her a medical report stating Shaghaf had gone mad two years earlier. They released her. She could have simply refrained from casting a predetermined "Yes" vote, like the rest of the family had. But she wanted to tell us the story of "No." In another instance, she went to a bar with friends, and ran into an old friend with his girlfriend. She began flirting with him in front of her, hugging and dancing with him, and before long the quiet bar descended into protests, shouting, commotion, and laughter. Shaghaf told us the following day how her friend's girlfriend had lost her senses and began shouting all kinds of insults at her.

As we made our way back from the Felucca restaurant, I wished this damn disease were simply about trading one life for another.

*   *   *

Nana Helena also grew up with only a first name. We don't exactly know her surname. My mother's gaze wanders toward me, drifting aimlessly. I look away from her eyes and instead at the camera, in a useless attempt to draw her gaze toward it. "Ghouzi… maybe her surname was Ghouzi…" my mother says evenly, with a shade of doubt. I envy her in that moment. Even without knowing her mother's surname, she'd had two loving parents and a milk-scented childhood! Like her sister Marianne, my mother grew up unburdened by fatal affiliations, nicknames, and identities. Nana had been in her twenties, maybe. Certainty has no place in this story. Every detail happened, maybe; nothing happened for certain. But it did happen, even if just maybe. I don't know how to explain it. Her uncle was Theodosius the Third, Patriarch of Antioch and the rest of the East. She went to him after giving birth to her first daughter, Marianne, and entrusted the child to her mother. He helped her reach northern Syria, where there were many centers for survivors, and where she searched desperately for her husband, whose name we don't know either. I'm not certain she was desperate. But she headed to northern Syria, of that we are certain, searching for her husband or a thread that would lead her to him. I can imagine her describing him in great detail, hoping to jog the tired survivors' memories. And I can imagine her standing silently in the face of their questions. Did she know her husband's name, or had she obliterated it the moment she lost him? Helena had tasted the bitterness of loss from a young age, when she lost her father. In her mind, this abandonment was cruel. Even though she knew he was ill with a terminal disease, in a sense he had abandoned her. The anguish of loss descended on her soul and settled there. It became part of her genetics, so much that she passed loss on to us. We all lived without a father, except for my mother, who didn't lose hers until relatively late in life. But when she lost him, she forged ahead with losing others. Or perhaps my grandmother's father, whose last name we aren't sure of, took the family's share of men with him. My father teased my mother one time, saying: "You're a family that devours its men." Big Mama's husband had passed away, and before that *her* father had also passed young. Nana Helena lost her father and her first husband. Aunt Marianne lost her father and husband. My mother lost her father and husband... and so on. The third generation of women lost only the fathers, though it had "devoured" the husbands. Nana, who had grown up with only a first name, was fortified by loss. As if the loss of her father had forced her to create the image of a man in her life, and since it was only an image, it belonged in her soul. Her father became a shadow who accompanied her wherever she went and gave her strength. She began searching for her husband, living or dead. She wanted to know, but she never did.

By chance, she met a handsome man. She was enchanted by his smile; it spilled from his lips and pooled on one side. She told him she was from the al-Harbiyat area, that her name was Helena, and that her husband was gone forever. He liked her fortitude and her broken Arabic mixed with Turkish, which rang like music in his ears. He was from a conservative family in Damascus, and Helena seduced him and stole his mind. "My name is Joseph," he said. He told her many stories and spoke to her without looking at her. His gaze wandered right and left as he told her interesting tales, to the point that Helena imagined he was speaking to himself, that she was in a dream, and that there was no Joseph before her at all. A few months later, they were married with her uncle's blessing, and moved to the al-Afeef area in Damascus. There she learned his name was Yousef, not Joseph, and that he was Muslim, not Christian. She only ever met his younger sister Bidrea. The entire family cut him off (in my grandfather's case, "the whole family" is accurate here) because he had married a Christian woman. They stopped visiting him. And Helena became Joseph's (or Yousef's) entire family. They lived in a house in al-Afeef until they passed.

My mother doesn't know where to start the story. And I'm lost along with her, in these scenes pulled from another time. She begins playing Shaghaf's game that night in Felucca, when she took refuge in the past from what she was experiencing now and what was to come. My mother also has two lives. Our everyday life and her memory, which bounces between times in her past, sometimes returning to her childhood and sometimes wishing the clock would go back just three years—if only we could go back to this temporary home we had in Beirut. It's true she complained often in those days, but at least the whole family was still there to hear her. She complained, grew angry, and sometimes cried. Then she would wish the clock could go back two years. Or even just one year. I feel helpless. How can I make up for all the others? I think about all the personalities we lived among. Some of us compensated for others' absences. But me, with my desiccated body, all I can do is listen. Me, who had made a mistake when I stole her from Beirut. I wasn't thinking; I never think. I'm afraid of thinking about things that may turn into more than I can handle. I hurriedly gathered our things, with closed eyes and a weary memory. I took her to the nearest airplane without her knowing. I didn't give her enough time to think, object, protest, or refuse. I knew that giving her enough time would allow me time to pause too. I didn't want to give myself a moment to take stock, that could change all the plans. I gave her just enough days to pack her memories in cardboard boxes. The entire house turned into a cardboard box, where we tossed our things after wrapping them with care. I'm haunted by the image of those boxes. That confusion and chaos makes me feel like I'm nowhere. The mover finished closing the final box and began carrying them all out to the truck. Our memories were leaving, one after another, in numbered boxes with simplified descriptions of their contents. How could we travel without memories? We would arrive in London two or three weeks before them! But having our memories depart in boxes made things easier. My mother became more relaxed when her belongings were taken from her and stuffed into these boxes. She may as well have been sleeping that last week in our Beirut house, she didn't absorb what was coming. How could she comprehend anything when her mind had traveled to the port of Beirut, along with mine, on a cargo ship voyage that would take weeks? Yes, without her knowing, I stole her from her quietude. To me, she was quietude itself, and wherever we came to rest, that quietude would come with us. I've made mistakes, a few, and can't admit those to her. I snatched her from a place where there still was a way to return, a place where if memory spills over, fear won't disturb the flow. And I've cast her here, where there's no way to trace a route back, where memory is so painful there's no point in recovering any of it, not even a whiff. This time my mother looks at the camera, as if wanting to absolve me from listening to what I've heard again and again, or perhaps entreating someone else, since she's lost hope in me, me who has been unable to help. She talks about how she longs for her pantry. She misses the creaking sound of her right pantry door. And her belongings arranged with care in drawers and on shelves, giving off a lovely smell. My mother excels at arranging her belongings. No wrinkles crease the clothing she irons with the utmost care, just like her tight and tidy face. I could never be so organized and precise. I've tried hard, but that kind of organization requires a patience I don't possess. So I've stopped thinking about my pantry and my belongings. I've become like Shaghaf, moving lightly without memory. I don't want to remember the past, not even yesterday. Meanwhile, my mother misses the creaking sound and says her eyes miss staring at a place filled with successive layers of time. She remembers the history of her every belonging. She's terrified by the idea that time has stopped in that pantry. Nothing new has been placed there for six years, perhaps longer! In longing for her pantry, my mother longs for what is missing from her memory. Neither her memory nor the story can continue without returning to her belongings, contemplating them, deeply inhaling their scent. As I listened to her words, terrible pain gripped my soul and squeezed hard. If only I could transport her to her room, to the little tile in front of the pantry door. If I could just give her the creak of the door opening, the whole world would unfold before her eyes, and that fragrant smell would seep into every pore of her weary soul. The most difficult type of longing is for things that are no longer there. How can I convince her that even if I were able to take her to that room, she wouldn't find what she's longing for? That room is not an isolated place tucked amid walls, houses, alleyways, and streets. You wouldn't find your city the way you left it, Mother... I began repeating that sentence again and again, until it echoed in my mind. Maybe I repeated it to ease my heavy feelings of guilt and impotence. Even though the words were true, they didn't absolve me of the mistake. I've made mistakes, some of them critical, and I can't admit those to her. The feelings of guilt don't soften them, either.

The alarm rang at five a.m. We had fallen asleep at three in the morning... or maybe not at all. Each of us in her own room. I remembered the day my father had passed away. We had also gone to his bed at three a.m. and woken up at five. Even though the alarm clock didn't ring that day, we woke at five, opening our eyes all at the same instant, not one after the other. I rose from my bed heavily; it wasn't the first time I'd woken so early, gone to the nearby bathroom, washed my face and looked at myself in the mirror. That trip: I had taken it often in the past. The same time, same taxi, a British plane taking me to London at the same moment. But this was the last time. I rose from bed, not thinking it would be the last time. I didn't want to think. I washed my face and looked into my eyes in the mirror for a long time. I stared at them for longer than usual. As if I wanted to leave behind some part of them on that surface above the sink. I truly needed to leave part of myself. We departed the house at six. For the entire hour beforehand, we didn't meet each other's eyes. Each of us was busy gathering herself, her belongings, and her emotions. Each of us was fumbling through a carefree house in Clemenceau, through a now-empty space that until recently was filled with them, with their commotion of various sounds, coming to visit us and become once again, even if for just a few days, "the whole family." I shut the door. Kept the key, as if the house were mine. I'd left behind lots of my belongings, furniture, and clothes. Part of my soul had to remain there, something that would prompt me to return for it. Only in the plane, during takeoff, did we look at each other. The blurred sight of my mother gazing at me from the other side of tears. I wiped my eyes to see her clearly and ladle up her comfort, but it didn't work. Her eyes were absent too, behind two pools of tears submerging her honey-colored pupils.

She was seventeen at the time, and on her way back from school. She was wearing a short beige skirt that revealed her slender legs, and a white blouse whose sleeves barely covered her shoulders. Her hair was long, her locks coyly tossed over her schoolbag. Like a butterfly she ascended the steep road that went from al-Taliani to al-Afeef and al-Muhajireen, walking lightly on tiptoe. A Fiat car stopped by her. The driver peered out the window with his big bald head and hooked nose.

"How're you, sweetie?"

"I'm good"' she replied, smiling.

He asked her if she wanted to be on stage.

"Me?"

He showed her the theater, and she promised she would ask her parents, and come back if they agreed.

"Just like that?" I asked my mother that evening. We weren't sitting at home, one on one, with the camera listening too. We were in a nearby coffeeshop overlooking the main street, watching passersby and enjoying observing the thrum of life separate from us. My question about how simple it was wasn't new. All of my mother's stories about her childhood, teenage years, and young adulthood prompted a similar question. All the details were simple, as were the social and familial relationships, sickness and death, love and life and war; even adoption was simple, no need for much deception or forgery. Then "the Baathists came," as people said, and even the simple act of breathing became incredibly complicated. When I was a child, the phrase "the Baathists came" conjured an image in my mind. I heard it in our living room, and in the living rooms of my father's friends, and I imagined a group of men wearing sky-blue uniforms made of shiny fabric, men with thinning hair so plastered to their heads by sweat that it looked like part of their scalp. I imagined them entering the city en masse, with evenly paced steps. My mother's child-hood wasn't under the brunt of this phrase. From an early age, I was aware of the vast space that yawned between our childhoods. I lived through the eighties and nineties relying on their time, or what remained of it, so as to survive my own depressing time. My father and I would make our way to Cham Palace Hotel or Omaya Hotel to meet his friends. The few paces between the taxi and those places may as well have been the chasm between two worlds, two eras. We went to the hotel lobby where plush velvet sofas and a wide glass facade ran the length of the coffeeshop. I always sat with my back to the street, to the dismal present time. I sat there with them, in their time, enjoying conversations I didn't under-stand much of. I was running, out of breath, longing to grow up quickly, and anxious for time to pass. I was well aware that if I were to take the ordinary amount of time to grow up, I would arrive there alone, without them, their conversations, or what remained of their era. In the taxi, my father and I took refuge in the big houses we passed; we peered into their lit windows and into the lives of those who lived there, imagining them sitting in front of the television, eating their dinners in silence, or maybe laughing. I discovered my father's hatred for the street and our dismal time. Like me, he was also running away, to the nearest window we came across. We soared through our idea of life, not actual life. Until my father grew weary of inventing that imaginary space, and passed on.

My mother, who dreamed of becoming a fashion model, tore down the road that thrilling afternoon, eager to arrive home and convince her parents. She ran holding Ragaa al-Giddawy's hand, pulling it to keep up with her, looking at her through eyes teary with joy. Ragaa was eight years older than her, and the first Egyptian fashion model, then professional actress. My mother had ripped her photo out of *Eve* magazine and hung it on the wall beside the window overlooking the balcony: Ragaa is standing with a straight back, wearing a tight and fancy sleeveless dress, turning her head to the right so that her long face with its delicate features appeared in profile. Kohl traced along the length of her eyelids. The tailor appears behind Ragaa, nearly as tall as her, putting the final touches on the dress before she sets off to model it. Her hair is short and thick. She doesn't look at us so much as she casts a glance across, without the slightest interest. This picture of Ragaa reminds me of a picture of my mother. In it, she is also standing indifferently, waiting for the makeup artist to finish her kohl-lined eyes with their long lashes. Also preparing for a theater performance. My mother was out of breath when she arrived home. She left Ragaa by the wooden threshold and entered the house at a run, this time like a flurry of butterflies, not only one. My grandmother's voice rang out through their spacious Damascus house, colliding with the salon's walls and receding from others, escaping and seeping into the little courtyard, colliding with the dining room walls, before bursting into the rooms above. "You want to act, do you?" Nana asked her screaming, the "ou" at the end of the word lasting as long as her breath could. Then she inhaled and began screaming again. According to Nana Helena, acting meant actors hugging and kissing, and that meant breaking all social bounds and traditions. My grandfather, meanwhile, had no objections at all. He took my mother by the hand, the same hand that had been holding Ragaa al-Giddawy's moments earlier, and left with her. My mother showed him the "theater," in reality a rented foyer in the Central Boycott Office not far from their home. Above the door to the "theater" were words my mother proudly read aloud: "Dramatic Arts Ensemble." My grandfather rang the doorbell. The man with the big head and hooked nose opened the door, smiling when he glimpsed my mother standing next to her father, herself smiling coquettishly. He offered my grandfather a handshake and introduced himself: Rafiq al-Sabban.

From then on, my mother went to the theater every day after she returned from school. She studied there, the other actors often helping her with her homework, and afterward trained in acting. My mother once introduced me to Rafiq al-Sabban, when I was a young child. We ran into him by chance near the Cham Palace Hotel. He hugged my mother with great feeling, and playfully pinched my cheek: "I raised your mother." At the time, I didn't understand what the phrase meant.

A few months after she joined the Dramatic Arts Ensemble, my mother took the stage at the Military Theater and gave her first performance: as Lady Macbeth.

My mother tells these stories like someone recounting a dream from the night before. This time, she casts her gaze away from me and toward the street. Lost in that limpid memory. I look into her eyes, consumed by guilt again. A mixture of guilt, fear, and powerlessness. If only I could carry her back in time. Twice my mother was stolen from her time: once when she met my father, and once when she met me. We discovered her quietude, and so we held on to her, we who were fraught with anxiety by heredity. We gathered her inside us, indifferent to her spirit so resistant to all shackles. We were engrossed with her completely: her memories, time, and past. We suggested to her that *we* were memory, time, and the past. And my mother, so gentle in temperament and mood, was convinced. She loved my father; she was crazy about him. She stepped away from the irresistible hubbub of the stage, television screen, and radio. She left all the fame she had worked for over years—with her distinguished voice, her incredible acting abilities, her gentle and strong presence—and took refuge in us instead. But in reality, we were the ones who took refuge in her. I imagine us holding on to her shoulders, being calmed by her quietude, letting her carry the worries of the entire world, and relaxing in her embrace. How did my mother reach this time? How did she arrive with two hands, two legs, a head, two eyes, and that sweet spirit still pulsing through her, even if only by great effort? Sometimes I wish she hadn't married my father. Instead married any man she met before him. I know that if she hadn't, I never would have met either of them. One day I returned from school to find my father ill, having spent most of the day in bed. My mother opened the door, smiling as usual. She didn't know that I had been standing behind the door for several minutes before ringing the bell. I was taking my time before coming home. Trying to eavesdrop, because I was afraid of feeling all at once. My mother didn't know that when she opened the door for me, her acting abilities manifested, faded, and finally, vanished completely. Every day, the same smile. A smile that sought to send reassurance into my heart, even though I could tell the difference between the truth and lies it held. On that day, her smile was different, it had no room for truth or lies. A smile fleeing from another time, not only drawn on her lips but shining from her roaming eyes. I went to the kitchen and put down my school bag, which was as heavy as the phrase "when the Baathists came" and heard a female voice escape my father's room. "Do we have guests?" My mother nodded. I ran into his room, and hugged him the way I did every day, then shook hands with the strange woman. Her voice was thin and obtrusive, and her laugh lacked kindness. I went back to my mother, whose smile still shone from her eyes. She uttered a single simple comment: "Pretty? She could have been your mother." I hugged her and told her that she was my mother and the most beautiful woman in the world. I wasn't lying.

an excerpt from the novel Suduf

DIARY OF
A CEMETERY

by FADI AZZAM

translated by GHADA ALATRASH

ACKNOWLEDGMENTS: A warm dedication and salutation
to the amputated arm in Mustafa Taj Aldeen Almosa's
"My Names Between the Hospital and Eternity"

*Ever since I laid my hands on these papers, I've had a strange feeling
about them. So, I decided to investigate deeper, relying on my modest
experience at the National Library. There was no signature on this
mysterious manuscript titled "Diary of a Cemetery"; only the ambig-
uous credit to "a former martyr."*

*The first pages of the manuscript were completely damaged and
corroded, but after a great deal of effort, we were able to salvage the
content shared in this document.*

The manuscript read as follows:

As we arrived, the place was teeming with confusion. I awaited my turn calmly. They took away all my things. Anxiously, but painlessly, I entered. As I became familiar with the place, my memory also gradually rid itself of its loads. Before long, what remained were only a few vivid images, which carried no meaning.

The next few pages were damaged and unreadable. Then, the handwriting became clearer:

DAY OF THE MARTYRS

May 6, 19? [*Note from the investigator: The year here is unclear but seems to date back to the past century.*]

Today, the living were busy organizing a celebration to commemorate our deaths as martyrs. Since early morning, my fellow martyrs in the cemetery have been living in a state of chaos and confusion. The cemetery remained noisy all day long. My fellow martyrs discussed the idea of filing a petition to protest the abuses committed by the cemetery guard. We could no longer tolerate his intrusive acts; his most recent victim happened to be my neighbor in an adjacent grave. As one of the oldest residents in the cemetery, he was greatly respected by everyone. We awakened to the news that his skull had been stolen and sold to medical students. [*Note from the investigator: The looting and trading of skulls is popular in our country, although it is a bold act considering the fact that graves are excavated and bones are exhumed. In the nineties, healthy skulls were sold in the US for ten to fifteen dollars.*]

I felt a great sense of loss and emptiness. He was truly a great neighbor who kept me entertained and helped me get through my first few days at the cemetery as I dealt with armies of worms, my flaking skin, the decay of my flesh, and the coagulation of my blood. It was also he who brought me to the awareness that the end of the journey is here in the cemetery and not the sky—indeed, a strikingly painful realization, but one we all got used to as the days went by.

But now, after the theft of his skull, he was no longer able to speak. That damn guard stealthily opened his grave and stole his head (I mean his skull) and left him helplessly floundering about the cemetery.

A VISIT

I visited the west side of the cemetery and was horrified when I heard the teeth-chattering-like noises that came from one of the younger martyrs (we martyrs chatter, for we are not able to cry tears). His chatter continued to escalate into an uproar and brought everyone to also chatter in deep sadness.

The fact of the matter was that our young martyr simply missed his wife and little boy. They visited him every year at this exact time and laid flowers on his gravestone, while the son would recount funny events to his father as he lay buried underground.

The commander of the young martyr's old unit was always eager to partake in this special occasion. He would stand next to the grieving mother and child, rubbing the boy's hair with his right hand as he groped the ass of our young martyr's wife with the other.

The noise of ceremonial cars sent chills down our bones as the clamor escalated. Nothing disturbed us more than the crowds of people and their emotions on this day.

A HISTORIC DECISION

We decided to boycott the ceremonies and wrote a petition to protest our miserable conditions. We couldn't find anyone but the cemetery guard to deliver our petition to the top leadership. In return for doing us this favor, the guard asked that we dispense with seven hip bones, five healthy skulls (unpunctured by any bullets or shrapnel), three collarbones, two ulnas, and one vertebral column.

A MARTYR WITH ONE ARM

I happen to be writing this diary with the bone of my right index finger that I dip in a mixture of clay I made myself. Oh, I've forgotten to inform you that I am a martyr with one arm. My left arm was lost to a mortar shell and was ripped from my shoulder.

A DEAL

While spring-cleaning my grave, I came to find out that everyone, including the guard of the cemetery, agreed (I will avoid using the term "conspiracy") that my body would be used to return the favor of delivering our petition.

In all honesty, I didn't mind the deal as it meant that I would soon visit the College of Medicine, a place filled with beautiful girls who would feel my bones.

A NEW ARM

They placed me on the autopsy table with reverence. The professor was not pleased to see my missing arm and yelled angrily, "I told you I wanted a whole body!"

The assistant ran to the storage room and brought back a new arm. He attached it to my shoulder. It felt different to the touch. Its fingers were thin and soft. It was a lost arm, stolen from a grave, exiled from its own body.

I felt it as it moved, pulsating with the heat of its memory. It moved slowly as if it wished to hold my right hand. The sensations aroused me, and I began to chatter uncontrollably, which in turn led to a state of panic in the room.

HEADLINES FROM OFFICIAL NEWSPAPERS

- *Al-Baath* newspaper reported that an incident at an anatomy lab caused "a state of fear and alarm among medical students when a skeleton began to move on its own and make chattering-like noises." In her comments about the incident, the dean of the College of Medicine dismissed the matter as a silly joke between old and new students, and vowed that those responsible for the chaos would be held accountable.

- *Al-Thawra* newspaper reported that "an incident that took place at the College of Medicine has led to the discovery of an organized network of people, headed by the guard of a cemetery, who sell corpses and body parts. The culprit, B. H. A., has been referred to the Office of Public Prosecution and charged with breaching trust and forming a gang to dig up graves."

- *Tishreen* newspaper further elaborated that "the incident has uncovered negligence and corruption in the Cemetery of Martyrs and has led to the dismissal of a high-ranking official after it was discovered that the remains of martyrs had been stolen. Formal authorities have intervened, warranting that the stolen remains would be returned to the cemetery in an official and ceremonious procession."

A SPECIAL CELEBRATION

By way of atonement and reparation, a new spacious grave was created for me. Above the grave was a large and hideous monument in the shape of a helmet with the inscription "Here lies an unknown soldier who has sacrificed everything for the sake of a homeland." Heaps of fresh wreaths were piled on top of the grave before the crowds departed solemnly.

After the celebrations ended, I felt a sense of pride and slept soundly for the rest of the night. In the morning, I was awakened by the sound of a herd of goats nibbling at the wreaths on my shrine. I was grateful for the goats, for when flowers and garlands become moldy, they are known to cause us unpleasant allergies.

My colleagues were eager to visit and welcome me back. But they were filled with envy, not because of the wondrous journey I had taken, but because of my new arm. They raced to congratulate me and shake my female hand. To be honest, I did not like what was happening. The fact of the matter is that corpses also have their boundaries!

I never expected a visit from the Wiseman of the Chinaberry Tree. He was a highly respected martyr, and it has been said that he was the first to reside here in the cemetery. His grave was spacious and located under the giant chinaberry tree at the top of the hill. He seldom left his place.

We talked for a short while. He asked me about the living and their world and how things were. I recounted everything I saw. He was especially curious to hear about how the city was boiling with fear and anger, and of the latest talks about the protests that were taking place in neighboring countries and beginning to reach our borders. I told him that I noted many soldiers in the streets, as if a new war was about to break out. He then asked me about my arm, and I explained what happened. Before he left, he extended his left hand to shake mine. I didn't want to turn him down, as it was obvious that he, too, wished to touch it. I raised my new hand carefully to rest it in his old palm, allowing for the thunderous heat to flow into his body. At its touch, life seemed to return to him and he no longer looked exhausted and weary. But as he began to squeeze it, I felt annoyed and afraid, and I pulled it out of his hand with difficulty. Apologetically, he muttered, "I am not sure what has come over me!"

[*Note from the investigator: It should be noted that these events took place at the beginning of 2011.*]

FALLING IN LOVE

Within a few weeks of my return, I began to fall in love with my arm. When it touched me, I was able to escape this absurd perpetuation in which I was stuck.

As it timidly stroked my head and passed over my body with tenderness, I felt an explosion of euphoria that reminded me of the mysterious and breathtaking sensation of happiness I once experienced.

Each time I sat down to write, my new mischievous hand caressed the pages, but this time it dipped its fingers in the clay I used for writing and neatly sketched three words in the middle of the white page. Three words that sent a radiating aura of light from my grave; the three most beautiful words after which neither life nor death mattered: I love you.

NEW ARRIVALS

Today, my kind neighbor unexpectedly knocked at my door and informed me of a special meeting that I was expected to attend. He also informed me of the arrival of three new martyrs who would also be at the meeting, which would be hosted by the Wiseman of the Chinaberry Tree.

Before he left, he whispered to me that the Wiseman wished that I go alone, adding in a shushed tone, "without your left arm."

I fully understood these instructions, but my arm did not. It was angry and began to jerk and jolt uncontrollably. The more I tried to calm it down and express my point of view, the angrier it got. Then, suddenly and unexpectedly, it slapped me. I was enraged, and so I grabbed it, pulled it off, and threw it in the corner of my grave. It continued to twitch, scratch, punch, slap, and then it raised its middle finger at me, turned the back of its palm, and ceased to move.

I stroked it with my right hand and assured it that I would not be gone for long. I apologized for my short temper and explained that this was the first time I had been invited to attend an important meeting. It shivered a little. It looked perfectly beautiful, delicate, and soft, and in its anger it was perfect, pulsating with life. I promised myself that once I returned, I would never abandon it again.

THE HORRIFIC WORLD OF THE LIVING

"You are traitors and do not deserve to be here," scolded the martyred general as he addressed the three newcomers.

I entered quietly, shadowed by fear, unaware of what was happening.

There were thirteen invitees, martyrs of the highest order and some of the most respected in the cemetery. They were all residents of the hill, summoned by the Wiseman of the Chinaberry Tree to discuss an urgent matter concerning the newcomers.

The newly arrived were very young. They stood silently with their heads bowed, stupefied and dumbfounded. Apparently, they had all been shot in the back.

One of them was still drenched with life's anger. In a voice saturated with defeat, he addressed the assembly of esteemed martyrs who were sunken into a state of solemn silence: "You may not believe what I am about to tell you, but this is truly how it all happened. There was a gathering of people who chanted slogans against corruption. They were not armed. They were not enemies. They were our people. Our army commander ordered two of us to shoot at them. We couldn't do it and lowered our guns in protest. It was at that moment that we felt bullets hit us from behind. Our own leaders killed us!"

The enraged martyred general interjected, "Lies! You were definitely killed by enemies. I know our army well, and they would never kill their own sons." He then yelled at the top of his lungs: "And what about your colleague over there?"

All skulls turned to another one of the new martyrs. He was devastated, barely able to move. "I was a skilled sniper, stationed on top of one of the buildings, and ordered to shoot at the crowds of terrorists and traitors. They must have noticed me, for a group of them stealthily crept up from the back, knocked the gun out of my hand, and threw me from the top of the building."

The place broke out into an uproar as everyone argued and shouted.

The Wiseman settled the matter with a loud shriek that caused everyone to freeze. Even the birds on the chinaberry tree fled in fright.

He commanded: "As of today, it is forbidden to speak about the cause of killing, no matter the case. Anyone who arrives at the Cemetery of Martyrs will be welcomed. Life was already a struggle because of divisions and feuds, but we all know that there is nothing worse than this damned *Barzakh*! So let's not torment ourselves and make things worse than they already are."

* * *

MASS GRAVES

Trucks continued to arrive daily carrying new martyrs. This caused great havoc and turmoil as the numbers of dead doubled the population of our already confined and limited space.

Bulldozers dug new vile pits, while trucks dumped the new corpses under the supervision of the senior guard. The bodies were piled on top of each other, some were still alive, which terrified us, for there was nothing more dreadful than to have some among us with still-beating hearts.

Then trucks covered the layers of dirt. Strange stelae were erected on top and labeled: Q: B—H 77.

The quarter labeled "B" had seventy-seven holes in total. A record was kept of those who resided in each hole and the forehead of every skull was plastered with a number. These permanently marked numbers helped us quickly identify new martyrs. We began to call them the numbered dead, but as we gradually got to know them and speak with them, we offered them citizenship in the cemetery, as is the case for all refugees whose journeys begin with numbers. It was not long before they gained everyone's respect.

THE DEAD INTOXICATED

My prison has become a gathering place for some of my colleagues.

One damn martyr smuggled in a liter of arak from the warehouse where the trucks unloaded the corpses. The men who helped unload the corpses were able to complete their tasks only under the influence of arak.

One liter of arak was enough to cause division among the martyrs and split them into two camps.

The leader of the Camp of Atonements, as it was called, was led by a terrified martyr known to us as "the trembling martyr." He did not chatter like the rest of us. He was only terrified. I recall how during his early days, when armies of worms helped rid him of his delusions, he would sob uncontrollably.

In the other camp, martyrs would sing longingly for Damascus, although most of us were not born there, nor did we know the city well enough. But we all felt a strong sense of belonging to it. One night is enough for anyone to be enamored with Damascus—to lie in her arms, breathe her in, and listen to her noises indeed beguiles anyone into justifying all her cruelty.

Our songs would reach the city that was covered with smoke, enveloped in fear, and lay in a state of numbness. The songs arrived in the form of sighing winds that came from the west, climbed over Mount Qasioun, flew alongside the flocks of terrified doves and amid the crowds on the sidewalks of Al-Salhiyeh, and seeped through the cracks of bullet-ridden walls. The songs broke through the barriers and barricades, and circled around the homeless, lost, frightened, and hopeless.

Amid shrieks of the frightened dead and death anthems sung by those afflicted with nostalgia, it began to rain in Damascus, or so it appeared to us.

The skies rained everything in pieces—children, lizards, distorted bodies, colored scraps of paper, decapitated headless corpses, barrels...

As the strange torrents of rains stopped, the cemetery was transformed into a city full of the lost dead. Ever since that day, we never drank again.

Instead, during moonless nights, we would stealthily sneak into the empty city where exhausted residents were sleeping or perhaps fighting off insomnia. It was during one of these nights that we caught a glimpse of that frightening old woman, known as Madame War, whom we had been warned about by the Wiseman of the Chinaberry Tree.

MADAME WAR

After our return from those dreadful visits to Damascus, and during our long, lonely, and dark nights in the cemetery, we gathered around the old Wiseman and listened to him as he talked about Madame War.

He began, "Madame War was born at the beginning of humanity on the sidelines of paradise. Her life took a turn when that one historic event took place, and our ancestors were expelled."

It all started back when that forbidden fruit was eaten. We are not sure whether it was a pear, an apple, a banana, or even a peach. Perhaps no one will ever know, but what is certain is that the forbidden fruit was eaten by Adam and Eve after they were deceived by the serpent, which in turn led to the expulsion of humans from the Garden of Eden.

Then came the first human death committed at the hands of a brother, and we were told by a crow to bury our crimes underground. But what we did not know was that what took place above ground would continue to haunt us until the end of time.

It was then that Madame War approached the dying brother's body, breathed in his last breath, and tasted his blood. She felt intoxicated, like never before. Ever since, she was no longer in search of what to eat or drink, for mankind became her favorite meal.

Some welcomed her; others warned about her.

Presidents of countries and lords of servants announced to the rebels, "You want War? So be it."

The bereaved mother cried, "How can War not be something sacred when my son died because of it?" while the father asked: "But how can War not be filthy when my heart died because of it?"

Meanwhile, Madame War rubbed her rough and calloused hands together. Toothless, she laughed at the top of her lungs, filling the space with her foul breath that reeked of rotten body parts.

Everyone saw her as a clumsy and inept old woman. They thought they could throw her a few corpses and then shoo her away.

But this was not the case, for once Madame War arrived, she found her way among the peoples and in between them.

The more divided and weaker they were, the stronger she became. Said the old Wiseman: "Believe me when I tell you that those who long ago drowned in the abyss of nothingness are the most fortunate of all. Your deaths were honorable; you have been spared from living through this cursed war where a tyrant kills his own people and one brother shoots another."

"But how is our death different?" asked a drunken martyr.

The Wiseman paused for a few minutes, and then replied, "Because there was a reasonable and honorable cause behind your death; you refused to be bystanders and you defended your country against an enemy, not against your own brother.

"And now that you have made it here, despite the darkness of the place, you have also been freed from the illusions of that futile and disappointing life," he continued. "Love becomes the one antidote to the disease of War. Love cannot coexist in the same space as War, for when War penetrates, lays her eggs, and nests her genes, all is transformed from beauty to ruin."

He continued, "She tears her way into the lives of those looking for bread to feed their children. She poisons their food and salts their lives with her darkness. She pollutes their air and water until their lives fade away. Yet she remains in everything. Even those who manage to flee from her grip continue to hold her memory close to their hearts so that their children are also not able to forget. Indeed, it seems to be the case that every time Madame War arrives at her new destination, humanity turns a blind eye; a humanity that stands regretful at the ruins of that next place afflicted with this disease of

War; a humanity that sits and stares, stupefied by how a map of a country can be turned over, upside down, like a sacrificed animal hanging in a butcher's shop; a humanity that is skilled at doing nothing but counting the dead who have fallen at the hands of War; a humanity that is quick to document in photos the images of those running away in humiliation; a humanity that impotently watches as people are turned into great feasts on which a lowly world feeds; a humanity that mutely endorses that which is spiteful and malicious, watching as people are degraded and humiliated."

The Wiseman's voice softened. "Everyone will come to find out that no one is spared her pollution. Every soul in her presence will be contaminated. Their foreheads will be eternally stained with her smog."

He does not stop: "War survivors live the remainder of their lives looking for love. They arrive ashore only to be welcomed as war survivors, as ones who had been vandalized and damaged, sort of like a piece of junk, good for nothing but the junkyards of humanity."

The Wiseman paused for a moment, and then asked the attentive dead in the cemetery: "Is this the world you long for, you idiots? Let the living cling onto that which you were able to rid yourselves of; let them wander in the ruins of their misery. If you have loved ones, pray that they, too, are freed from their illusions and that they may quickly join you here in this limbo-inducing but true place. For once you are afflicted with war, you will never be able to feel peace again until you arrive at this cursed place, at this cemetery. I am warning you, all of you martyrs, stop going there; stop polluting our safe place with the viruses of nostalgia, do not kill us twice, do not expose us to the diseases of the living. Do not allow Madame War to find her way to this grind between remembrance and forgetfulness."

Suddenly a hoarse laugh broke out and disrupted the orderliness of the place. Everyone was astonished, some were resentful. He was one of the newly arrived martyrs, hysterically giggling and laughing.

Laughter was a curse and a bad omen in a cemetery—this is why the living kept silent when they visited. But now it was a dead man laughing.

Some of those who sat next to him tried to silence him by force, but the Wiseman intervened and asked that he come closer. He sniffed him, looking for traces of alcohol, but found none.

He asked, "How were you martyred?"

The laughter stopped. The martyr replied, "I swear I do not know. You can call it collateral damage. I was going to buy bread for my family when I suddenly found myself caught in the crossfire of two groups shooting at one another. The bullets fell like rain. I didn't know who stood against whom. When I woke up, I found myself here. But I am laughing because it isn't so bad here. My toothache has disappeared, and I am no longer hungry. I have escaped that disgraceful life. All my pain ceased at once." He looked at all the dead mockingly and said, "I can't understand your sadness. What life are you yearning for? Get up, celebrate, and dance, for you have escaped terrible torment; you have escaped that place, hell itself."

THE FINAL PAGE

Today, my lost arm returned, exhausted. It peacefully stroked my face with its fingers, reached for my notebook, opened the last page, and wrote this sentence, with which I will also end and bid you farewell:

"Once you have read this diary, let it be known that you are now forever cursed, until you break the silence over what has happened."

an excerpt from

BLOOD ON
THE MINARET

a novel by JAN DOST
translated by MARILYN BOOTH

THE WOUNDED FINGER OF THE LORD

THEY AWOKE THAT DAY, the people of Amuda—the little
Kurdish Syrian town that had been chucked down with
precise geometric measurement exactly two parasangs south
of where history's conflagrations erupted. The village reclined
in melancholy on a cushion of land stuffed overfull with the
mocking guffaws of geography's designs on humanity. On
the morning of the last Friday of June in the year 2013, the
townsfolk woke up to a horrific scene the likes of which they
had never witnessed.

They saw the minaret of the town's "grand mosque"
dripping blood. It was dripping from the long and narrow

apertures, which now looked like newly opened wounds on the slim, elegant form of the minaret. In the past, the call to prayer had always sailed outward from its pinnacle, depositing a sense of reassurance and security in the hearts of the believers—and also in the hearts of the town's beggars and tramps, the usurers and the slightly crazed, and the lazy, devil-may-care poets. That peaceful reassurance even infused the breasts of the town's doves. But the doves were absent from the bloody scene that faced the townsfolk on the morning of that June day.

People quickly gathered and circled around the base of the hemorrhaging minaret. The terror of what they saw rearranged their facial features according to its own caprices. Every face was turned upward, eyes fixed on the bright-red blood running down the pale-yellow sides of the minaret. At its pinnacle, a silver crescent moon reached toward the muted sky like an open mouth warning of disaster.

At first the blood came slowly, at a trickle, red threads descending from above. But soon the threads began to thicken and spread. Now the blood was gushing out until it covered the walls of the minaret entirely. Their mouths flopping open like copies of the mute crescent atop the minaret, the astonished onlookers could even hear the sound of spurting blood in the silence.

The onrush of sound might have reminded the more macho men in the crowd of what their own upright columns had shed, the night before, into the wombs of their prone sexual partners, after those Ashawis had shed the blood of tens of people demonstrating in the early evening for the release of their friends. Four demonstrators had died immediately from the volleys of the Dushka machine guns. Weapons experts had designed these heavy guns for the task of ripping apart the metal bodies of airplanes, not the tender flesh of human beings.

The "Ashawis" was the name the ruler over Syrian territory had given to his allies among the Kurds who protected his back and suppressed the defiant energies of the young in the north to keep them from getting drawn into revolutionary turmoil—that is, to prevent them from putting more wood on the flames that already burned and turning them into a huge bonfire. "Ashawis" combined an Arabic label with a term that Kurds had used to name a militia they formed—Asayish, meaning safety and security. That militia name had been derived from the region of Kurdistan that sat across from the region of death that those militiamen had inaugurated, laying its foundation stone in the town of Amuda itself.

Salih, the town's novelist, who had been kept awake for seven days and seven nights in his struggle with the opening to his new historical novel, was there among the bewildered crowd, his mouth hanging open as he stared, like everyone else, at the bleeding window slits. Turning, he saw the poet who frequented Amuda's lackluster cafés. The man always wore a red T-shirt and was called by town residents "the skinny poet." With one hand, he was attempting to fend off a persistent fly buzzing closely around his head.

Their eyes met—everywhere on the scene, people's bewildered stares locked with those of their neighbors as they flocked to the site. Novelist Salih was startled to hear a question that shot out of Skinny Poet's mouth like a volley from a Dushka machine gun.

Who wounded the minaret?

The novelist's silent response was to jerk his head upward—a head covered in long hair, two-thirds of which had gone white—as if he were pointing out an address to an inquiring person who lost his way. His eyes remained suspended on the ropes of blood, which had crawled further down the minaret by now, nearly reaching the ground, ready to touch down close by as the crowd stood transfixed.

Skinny Poet looked upward too, his mouth as wide open as the cavity of the brass pitcher with which a rather mysterious dervish who went by the name and title of Sufi Kunduru would do his ablutions on Fridays, always in the mosque courtyard, paying no mind to the weather and its incessant changes. He repeated his question in another form as he pointed to the erect minaret standing there tall and alone, a catastrophe like no other.

Who wounded this finger of the Lord? Who?

Salih the Novelist smiled, but it was a sad smile. He did admire the poet's eloquence—this fine metaphor he had found, one saturated in the sacred.

It is not Iblis—that's certain, he replied in a faint voice.

This made Skinny Poet angry, and when he spoke again, his voice was loud.

Did you see me accusing my Lord Iblis, lord of the poets, Salih? You know how deep our relationship goes. I am his disciple, man.

A satirical edge creeping into his voice, Salih responded with another question. So, then, why are you so concerned about the Lord and his fingers, since you're in such cahoots with your master Iblis?

The poet was infuriated. His angry voice got heads turning. Eyes which until that instant had been fixed on the rivulets of blood now swiveled to stare at him.

There's no war between the Lord and Iblis. No war, Salih, no war. You will not understand me, you're just a novelist of disappointment and failure, an incoherent mess!

With a quick light movement, he plucked off the sticky fly that had landed on the tip of his eyebrow, imprisoned it in his left fist, and turned his back to the crowd as he headed for the mosque yard.

FOUR SHORT STORIES

by RAWAA SONBOL

translated by KATHARINE HALLS

NO ONE TALKS TO THE OLD MAN

IT'S ARRIVED, DAD. YOU *can go and pick it up today.* Amin can hear the joy in his son Amer's voice. He replays the WhatsApp message he received early that morning, writes down the address that Amer gives, then begins his morning routine: he shaves carefully, drinks his coffee on the balcony among the leaves and blooms of the plants that were his wife's pride and joy, waters them and reads the fatihah for her soul, has breakfast, and finally gets dressed in a pair of carefully ironed black pants and a white cotton shirt with a fake Lacoste logo on the left breast. He looks himself over in the mirror, satisfied, then puts on a pair of sunglasses and a smart houndstooth cap with a leather trim. This is Amin's uniform of choice, to be worn each workday from seven-thirty to two; in such an elegant outfit he looks more like an air pilot than a taxi driver.

At seven-fifteen Amin leaves the house and begins the daily ritual of cleaning his car. He removes the mats from the footwell, shakes them out and replaces them, wipes the dust from the windscreen with a dry cloth, wipes down the seats with another, damp cloth, then takes his place at the wheel. The engine coughs and growls when he turns the key in the ignition, and the car shudders; Amin knits his neat white eyebrows and looks anxious, thinking that he can't be late, today of all days: he needs to be in town early to pick up the money that Amer has taken such trouble to send, to cover the cost of installing solar panels, the idea being that they'll give him a few hours' more electricity each day than the four the government provides, because sending money from the USA isn't easy: the citizenship interview that Amer's been waiting years for is coming up, so he hardly wants to provoke suspicious questions about an international bank transfer to an Arab state, and unfortunately this time he couldn't find a friend who could personally deliver the money to his father, which is what he usually does, though he asked around for two months; eventually a relative of a friend of his turned out to be going to the United Arab Emirates, and from there another person would arrange the transfer to Damascus for a brokerage fee calculated per each thousand-dollar increment.

That's the ticket, Fair Lady, says Amin gratefully as the car, sounding healthy again, pulls away. Fair Lady is a white Fiat 131 he purchased more than thirty years ago now, the nickname given by Amin's wife shortly afterward in teasing reference to the inordinate care he showed it having stuck; the other thing that's stuck to it—on the back of the driver's seat, to be precise—is a rectangular piece of paper, laminated in plastic, bearing his cell phone number and below that, in an attractive font, two words: Grandpa Amin.

Composing this sign involved long deliberation: he didn't want to put his full name, because it's a small world, and he might someday pick up a passenger who knew his son or daughter, and sooner or later they'd hear he was working as a taxi driver, and they'd definitely be mad, because Amer sends more than enough for him to live on. *How about Ustaaz Amin?* he pondered, but although he'd gone by this more formal title for years—from the time he was first employed at a department of the Ministry of Education up until his retirement—he ruled it out, because he didn't want people to laugh at him, or at best feel sorry for him. He finally settled on *Grandpa* because it befitted his age, seventy-three, and would inspire passengers with a sense of familiarity, and anyway he liked how the two words sounded together—*Jiddo Amin*—even if he does consider his grandpa status to be pending, seeing as he has five grandchildren but has never met them, except on his mobile phone screen, in irregular, truncated video calls, and doesn't know if he ever will.

* * *

No one talks to the old man. The phrase, which comes to Amin often, always raises a smile; it's based on the title of a novel by García Márquez, his favorite writer—*No One Writes to the Colonel*—and he always thinks that if he were the hero of a novel, this would definitely be the best title, because in truth it's Amin's need to talk to other people that has driven him back to work since his wife's death; only once he'd started did he realize that the money he made from the taxi was enough to sustain a simple, humble lifestyle, relieving him of the need to rely on the remittances his son insists on sending—so he can fill up the mazut tank at the beginning of winter, pay a woman to cook and clean for him three times a week, service Fair Lady, whom he'll never ever trade in, go for a full medical, and so on. Amin takes receipt of the money and assures his son that the mazut tank is full, the house is shipshape, Fair Lady's running like a hundred horses, and he himself is in rude health; but in fact he puts the money into an old shoe box, which he hides carefully under the bed and which he has just emptied—last week, in fact—because when today's transfer arrives he'll be able to pay the last instalment and complete the plan he's been working on since roughly a month after his wife's death, when his grief simmered down and he began to think, in practical terms, about himself.

Amin doesn't typically hide anything from his son and daughter, but this time he's had to act alone, because he knows they'll object—they just won't understand his need for company, for peace of mind—and this is what he's thinking about as he drives, slowly as always, through the suburban streets, until he reaches the main traffic circle, where he slows down and flashes his headlights at the people waiting, calling out *Damascus Damascus* as he approaches; since it's rush hour he won't have to wait long, and the car is soon full, four passengers who split the fare, and he pulls away, heading for the heart of the capital, where he'll drop them off, then have to search for a parking space, which will be tricky at this time of the morning, but he doesn't need to think about that now; he's going to make the most of the twenty-five-minute drive by talking to the passengers, though he can't always pull this off, because some passengers like to finish their night's sleep in the car, and young people these days are usually wired to their cell phones, headphones in, humming to themselves or grinning idiotically from time to time, and there are some passengers who prefer silence, and who, if Amin addresses them, simply nod and pretend to look out the window.

He has some tricks to get people to talk: sometimes he relies on the radio, flicking through the stations until he comes across, say, a morning sermon, allowing him to remark that men of religion are hypocrites and liars, because every passenger's got a story to support *that* view, or Fairuz's voice will ring out and he'll ask God to bless the souls of the Rahbani brothers and complain that songs these days aren't a patch on the old ones, and if he gets the news he'll listen for a moment, then sigh that *they've sold the country down the river, they've ruined it, and they're sitting on the trash heap that's left*. The passengers will agree and a thread of conversation will emerge, though when Amin chimes in to curse the government and the opposition alike, it will snap in fear and someone will say, *We ask God to bring relief*, in meaningful tones, and Amin will remember himself and change the subject. His favorite part is when he tells his own story, never hesitating to add some spicy details here and there to keep them interested, otherwise he'll find himself sitting there in silence, and goodness knows the hours he spends in silence at home are long enough, because his lifelong friends all died one after the other in the space of less than five years, and then suddenly his wife died too. He delayed the burial by two days so Dina could come from Germany. She came alone, didn't bring her family, and in the few days she spent with him she seemed like a stranger and grumbled about everything in the country, then left again; Amer couldn't manage the trip, but he waited until the funeral and burial were over, then suggested Amin sell the house and car and come to live with him in America. Amin refused emphatically. *I'm afraid of dying a long way from home*, he explains to the sixty-something man sitting in the middle back seat, who's listening with interest, *I want to die and be buried here*. The man agrees and Amin goes on, addressing him in the rearview mirror, to recount in detail how he found his wife dead in her bed one morning, and how lucky he was because he managed to have her buried in al-Dahdah cemetery, right in the center of the capital, and all he'd had to do was make one phone call to the eldest son of her brother, who'd passed away years ago. *Bury her in Dad's grave*, said the young man, *we're not coming back, alive or dead.* He told Amin the siblings were all amenable, and the matter was quickly arranged.

You're kidding! A grave in Dahdah goes for thirty million lira! exclaims the fifty-something man sitting next to Amin. *Forty actually, brother*, Amin corrects him confidently, and with that the topic turns naturally to inflation and the situation being so terrible, which is enough to keep the three men in conversation for the entire rest of the journey, while a woman in her forties dozes at one window and a university student leans against the other, engrossed in reviewing her lecture notes.

Amin drops off the passengers at President's Bridge and continues on his way, and an hour later he's picked up the remittance, already changed into Syrian lira; for the next week he's busy with phone calls and appointments, then he finishes off the procedures and the papers are signed.

These solar panels are a godsend, Amer. What a good idea. He's sitting in the bedroom by the light of a single candle as he says this to his son one weekend. He's hoping he'll tell him about many things, but he reminds himself the boy's busy, pragmatic, and at the end of the call, when his son asks him with genuine concern whether he needs anything, he absentmindedly opens a drawer near the bed and happily picks up the piece of paper he's obtained after visiting various agents and realtors. *No, don't worry about me, nothing at all*, Amin assures him, and in the dim light of the candle he can nevertheless make out the words on the document that bears his fingerprint and signature.

The Proprietors in exchange for valuable consideration, receipt of which is hereby acknowledged, do transfer to the Grantee, the exclusive right of burial at the premises described as follows: plot of 265 × 90 × 170 cm + 20 cm elevation, located in al-Dahdah Cemetery. The office located in permanence at the site can provide all requisites for the deceased and use of a hearse.

AMIRA WHO KNOWS

AMIRA KNOWS THAT SOMETHING different is going to happen today. She's known since she woke up, perhaps because she had a dream that her mind won't let her fully remember—she believes bad dreams need to be forgotten so that they don't come true—or perhaps it's because the first thing she saw in the garden that morning was a dove's nest blown to the ground by the night wind, her heart thumping when she saw the cracked egg and heard the mother's agonized cooing.

Amira, in her seventies now, knows many things, not because she's had any education—she can barely read, just a few words—and not because she has talkative neighbors who

visit or children and grandchildren who are always around—
she's been alone for years—and not because she has a TV to
keep her abreast of entertainment and news—she just has a
small transistor radio, which she inherited from her husband
twenty years ago, and sometimes she manages to pick up one
of the stations that broadcast pop music and horoscopes as
well as the hourly local news roundup, which tirelessly assures
listeners that all is well.

Amira, with her big bulky body, knows many things,
even though she rarely leaves her spot against the filthy wall
at the edge of the public garden. She sits permanently on a
large, tattered sofa beneath the words PUBLIC TOILET, which
are scrawled in large letters, and two wonky arrows pointing
toward the metal door, which remains ajar all day but which,
at night, Amira locks behind her on her way to the narrow
rusted frame that is her bed, inside the damp toilet block,
where she hunts down a few hours of rest if she's lucky, because
sleep takes flight at night, only to settle comfortably on her
head during the day, weighing down her eyelids and sapping
the energy from her body, so that she dozes off on the spot,
though nobody glancing at her from a distance would guess
she was sleeping, because her pose is so dignified: shoulders
straight, back resting on the back of the sofa that's held her
body these past two years; before that, she used to spend her
days sitting on a plastic garden chair, but one morning she
found the sofa abandoned among the aged trees that surround
the toilet block, and a single glance told her the whole story:

somebody had pulled the sofa from the rubble after a battle on the outskirts of the capital, and then, having failed to sell it in the Thieves' Market, had dumped it here in the garden, where Amira beat the dust from the upholstery, wiped it down with soapy water so its gold blooms gleamed against the blue background, carefully sewed up the tear in the back, glued the carved wooden ornament back in place, and finally threw away the plastic chair; the sofa became her friend.

Amira, with the long faded black robe that's belted below the waist, knows some things that might not interest anybody: she knows without moving from her seat, for instance, which bathroom stall is going to be used, by listening to the footfalls and the squeak of the door, and she knows that the men who visit her toilets are few and far between, because men have the luxury of relieving themselves in other locations, as the weary stones of the ancient city walls next to the garden can attest. She also knows that in the early mornings, nobody comes to the public toilets except similar-looking young women with tired faces and smudged eyeliner, and near-threadbare skin-tight clothes, the high heels of their decrepit shoes wobbling so wildly it looks like they're planning to detach themselves and scuttle away; she knows that it's hunger that drives them out of their homes, that the night draws them in and lures them down dark, narrow alleys, that the morning disavows them, that the city sticks its fingers down its throat and meanly vomits them up before the office workers and schoolchildren appear; yet Amira greets them with a kind, commiserating smile, and although they spend an age in the bathroom, Amira doesn't mind: after five years of this she knows that it's not just about a full bladder or heaving bowels or a pad that needs changing, because one of those girls, with the help of nothing more than lipstick, cheap eyeliner, and a cracked mirror on a grimy wall, can come out of an ugly place like this looking lovelier, and another can have a long intimate phone call that makes her body hot despite the unpleasant cold seeping from the walls; Amira also knows that a cramped bathroom stall is as good a place as any for a woman to set free the pain in her chest, no matter how huge. Amira loves these women— especially the young ones, who aren't even twenty yet—who deposit their secrets with her, who come to her when they're pregnant, for home remedies that will make them miscarry: Amira is generous with her knowledge, and because ginger and cinnamon sticks are expensive, she makes do with onion skins, which she boils for them herself.

Amira, with her wide, gappy smile, knows how to listen properly; she takes an interest in the stories of passersby who use her toilets, pulling at the coarse hairs on her chin while she listens, and is never stingy with the tea she prepares over a small stove at her feet, or indeed with sympathy or advice, but she does, however, know not to get too attached to anyone, because people come and go, and others come in their place—beggars and garbage men, bus drivers, office workers and street traders, night girls, soldiers, schoolchildren—while she alone remains, guarding the filthy toilets like the old trees guard the river Barada, which cleaves through the garden here. Amira wishes that somebody would stay with her, which happened on occasion in years past, when war rained down from the city's skies, and Amira knew that a strange deserted place like her public toilet could feel safe and familiar; Amira would be as happy as those toilet-block refugees were afraid, and when the stink brought looks of disgust to their faces, Amira would smile sadly, because she knew that that stink was the smell of the city, the whole city, and she knew it would make no difference as she hurried to shut the three toilet stalls, because as she always says, with the wisdom age brings: *You can keep things behind closed doors, but they'll find their way out in the end.* Amira knows that all sorts of things can wriggle out, like the thin line of blood that trickled out one time under the door of the third stall, where a rose of a woman in her twenties had slashed her wrists—she died and found peace, but Amira was summoned for lengthy interrogations, and spent the night at the local precinct—or like the shriek of alarm that came from the second stall, that time when a trail of something clear and viscous slid across the dirty tiles, and Amira opened the door to find a terrified face, round belly, and crossed legs, and realized the woman was about to give birth; some kind souls called the Red Crescent, but the baby was in a hurry, and it was Amira whose arms welcomed it joyfully to the world, Amira who cradled it tenderly to her breast and whispered the words of the azan in its ear, Amira whose clothes were stained with blood and goo and whose heart nearly burst with happiness, because she hadn't known until that moment whether she would ever hold a grandchild to her bosom, because Muhammad was long gone—Muhammad her one and only, Muhammad her heart's joy and anguish.

Amira knows her work inside out: she unlocks the metal door early in the morning and wedges it open with a rock; she takes one hundred lira from each visitor in exchange for a smile and a gesture indicating they can go on in; she isn't too wasteful with her toilets' share of the cleaning products the municipality hands out every few months, only cleaning when the filth becomes unbearable, but every night before going to sleep she makes a circuit of the toilets with a bleach-soaked cloth and checks each stall in turn, carefully examining the walls and the inside of the doors, because she knows that people leave things behind, they draw hearts and lips and signatures, they write crude phrases and cell phone numbers with names—Amira takes care never to erase the numbers, because one day she'll buy a cell phone, and then she'll call these numbers, one each day, and though she doesn't know what she'll say, she's certain she'll find plenty to talk about with people who must be as lonely as she is—but anyhow the names and numbers really aren't a problem, the real problem is those phrases she comes across from time to time: she laboriously unpicks the words, and when she's understood what they say she can't stop her hands from trembling as she scrubs them away in fright, for Amira knows that just one of these sentences is enough to guarantee her a place in a dark underground room. She finds other phrases too, and she usually ignores their vulgarity, because she believes that God doesn't have dark underground rooms and is too great to be perturbed by some blasphemy scribbled on a toilet wall in a moment of despair; and because she believes, too, that He is by nature merciful, she doesn't bother scrubbing them off until Ramadan approaches.

Amira knows many things, including some she wishes she didn't know; like everyone here she'd heard a lot about the dark underground rooms, but five years ago she memorized them, visited them all while looking for Muhammad before finding out he'd been swallowed up by the one with the worst reputation of all, and today, just before nine in the evening, a skinny pale young man shows up carrying a bag of bananas and another of apples, says hello, goes awkwardly into the toilet, then comes out a few minutes later looking like someone relieved of a heavy burden and gives her everything all at once: plastic bags, a few laconic words, and a small key. *Say God is one, Auntie*, he says in a trembling voice, his eyes filling with tears as he rubs her on the shoulder, and that's enough for Amira to know.

Amira knows many things, but she ignores them sometimes, tricks herself; she knows that the war crushed her home, leaving a heap of rubble in its place, a few months after Muhammad disappeared, and that these toilets are her home now, but still she's glad to have the key to the house, and hides it between her large, sagging breasts; she knows equally that Muhammad died two years ago, because that's what she was told by the skinny young man who was in there with him, and who spent three months looking for her once he got out, and yet she beams when she sees Muhammad as the dawn azan sounds, and when he holds out a hand, she takes it and gets up, and now Amira knows that although her body is there on the bed, she has Muhammad's arm through hers, and she's going with him, and she doesn't need to worry.

HE DIDN'T COME BACK

After Pirandello

I.

LOOK, BY THE WINDOW, squealed the boy mischievously. The Damascus-Homs bus was about to leave, full except for the seats at the back, so he scampered down the aisle in his bulky jacket, all of five years old, and clambered into the window seat on the righthand side, the other passengers registering the contrast between his excitement and energy, and the composed, downcast appearance of his mother, a handsome woman in her thirties wearing an old but presentable coat, who followed him with deliberate steps and a straight back.

The boy glued his face to the glass and gazed out curiously at the people in the bus station. His mother, meanwhile, was indignant at the sight of the four empty seats in the back, because if she'd known, she could've bought one ticket instead of two and saved herself a whole three thousand lira by putting the boy on her lap, but she always bought two tickets so that she and her son could occupy two seats, as her husband insisted, not out of any concern for her comfort, but out of long-distance jealousy, this aspect of his personality having assumed pathological proportions since he'd gone abroad. *You won't relax until you've found a genie's lamp to keep me and my son in.* She fixed her headscarf and smiled wryly, remembering what she'd said when they argued yesterday, after she told him she was going to use the three-day school vacation to visit her family, and her chest clenched as she contemplated the abyss that separated them, but soon the driver had taken his place at the wheel, and she breathed a sigh of relief, because the seat next to her was still empty and this was good, not only because it meant she wouldn't have to lie when her husband interrogated her, but because the filthy mood she'd been in since yesterday did not dispose her to put up with any small talk.

The driver turned the key, started the engine, and closed the door; an elderly man in the front seat muttered the travel prayer; a young man in military uniform closed his eyes and inclined his head ready for the nap he'd been looking forward to; a girl in her twenties smiled as she sent a WhatsApp message—*Just leaving the station babe*—and in fact they were meant to be just leaving the station, but a series of raps on the metal side of the bus at that very moment were to ensure that it stayed where it was for a good twenty minutes more.

Going to Homs? The rough, brassy voice entered the bus first, followed by its owner, a woman in her seventies, her right hand clutching the metal cane she'd just used to halt the bus; the left hand was pulling along a girl of five, who in turn was carrying a large plastic bag.

Yes, Auntie, Homs, but I'm leaving now, said the driver, explaining that she'd have to go to the ticket window and buy a ticket for the next departure. The passengers could all hear as the woman argued with him; the young woman in the back seat was following, bored, and because she liked things to be neat and tidy, she'd started imagining she could tuck the woman's big belly in, do up the buttons of her shabby, too-tight coat, tie back the loose locks of orange-shaded peroxide-blond hair, and straighten the small floral-print scarf on her head; she smiled in satisfaction at the thought of the end result, though it became a grimace when she heard the woman say: *I'll go with you or nobody, I've taken a shine to you.* The driver smiled, defeated. *Bless you, Auntie*, he said and asked his helper to take the woman's ID and run back to the office to register her name and buy her a ticket, but at this the woman raised her eyebrows and pursed her bright red lipsticked lips. *What if you lose it?* she accused the helper, and he promised her he wouldn't, swearing by his moustache, his eyes, and the Holy Qur'an, but still she refused to hand it over. *You're not going anywhere without me*, she said to the helper, and at this point the driver was losing his patience and some of the passengers were grumbling and tutting, but the young man gave up. *Let's go then, Auntie*, he sighed, and she, radiant with victory, said, *God be pleased with you*, and got off the bus behind him, trailing the little girl even though the driver suggested she stay on the bus to wait. *Heaven forfend!* she said, *I'm not letting her out of my sight.*

The trip to fetch the tickets and back took over a quarter of an hour, and by the time the woman returned everyone on board was glaring and infuriated, but she beamed at them and made her way to the back seat with her granddaughter, smiling at the little boy's mother, who gave a brisk, insincere smile in response; when the granddaughter smiled at the little boy, however, he grinned back at her and quickly abandoned his own seat so as to sit next to his new friend, which under usual circumstances would have pleased his mother, because it meant she'd get a break from his demands for the duration of the journey, but seeing as the older woman was now sitting right by her, it wasn't looking good, and sure enough, the woman had barely sat down and still had her head inside her large, overfull fabric purse, one hand rooting around for her cell phone to hand to the girl, when the younger woman heard the first question, immediately followed by others: name, age, where she was from, where she was going, what her husband's name was, why he'd gone abroad, was he settled now? The younger woman leaned close to the window, trying to keep her distance from the older woman and the pungent smell of her sweat, and responded curtly to her questions, thinking that this interrogation had to be the worst thing that would happen today, not knowing that the older woman would later accidentally sneeze in her face, crunch on potato chips right by her ears, or drink by mistake from her bottle of water, and not knowing, either, that she, the young woman, would be beset again and again by an urge to push the older woman out the window.

2.

This was the first time the older woman had taken the bus to Homs, though it surely wouldn't be the last. *I won't deprive you of your daughter*, she'd said to her daughter-in-law three months back, *I swear to God I'll bring her if I have to carry her on my head*, and she wasn't one to break a vow, not while her heart was still ticking, she'd take the girl to see her mom whenever she asked, she'd take her if she had to crawl to Homs on all fours, she assured the young woman next to her, of course telling her the full story: how her son had gone missing five years ago, along with the little pickup he delivered vegetables in, how they'd asked and asked, and waited and waited; *He just... dissolved. Like salt*, she said, slapping one palm against the other to demonstrate: not a trace. Months went by, and his wife gave birth to her daughter, then years went by, and the girl got older, and last year the older woman's husband had passed away. Her kids had insisted they put the family house on the market. She'd gone to the Islamic court where the judge ruled the missing man should be considered dead, so his brothers split the inheritance from the house, the older woman moved into a smaller place, and the daughter-in-law came to spend her waiting period there. All this the older woman recounted neutrally, like she was explaining the plot of a TV series. *That's how things go*, she concluded. *The living have to come before the dead, my girl.* She fell silent for a moment, but before the younger woman had time to offer a kind remark, or invoke mercy for the son's soul, the older woman leaned toward her and added in a whisper: *After the waiting period was over, she went to visit her family and never came back—they married her off to somebody there and made her leave her daughter with me.*

Mama got married! said the girl happily, having followed the conversation while appearing to be engrossed in playing on the cell phone with the boy. *That's right, sweetie*, said the older woman with a smile, *your mom is the prettiest bride*, then asked the girl if she was hungry, shoved her hand into her purse, and rummaged around before producing some olive oil and za'atar sandwiches and some cucumbers; the younger woman politely refused the offer to share, so the older woman handed the food to her granddaughter and the boy as well as eating some herself, then dozed off and began to snore loudly, and finally the young woman got some time to herself, but instead of thinking about her arguments with her husband, and how she wished he wouldn't be able to settle down and hoped the family reunification process would never happen, she found herself feeling sorry for the older woman and gazing at the back of her hands: the bulging veins, the crinkled skin and the liver spots, the swollen fingers, and lastly the red nail polish, which brought a smile to her face.

After an hour, the older woman woke up and became even more talkative, describing her late son in detail this time and recounting how he'd got married and how it took a long time for his wife to get pregnant, laughing as she told anecdotes about the shaykhs and doctors they'd visited and medication they'd tried, and the young woman listened, not because she couldn't push her out of the window, but because a fine bond of familiarity was beginning to form between the two women.

Goodness me, Auntie, the Lord made you strong, said the young woman kindly when the older woman finally stopped talking. *Thanks be to God*, said the older woman with a smile as she pulled the little girl into her arms. *I have Wafa' now. She's named after me, and she's so like my son, dear Lord, the spitting image!*

The girl was still tapping away at her game while squeezed in her grandmother's embrace, and without looking up from the cell phone screen, she said to the boy:

—*Where's your dad?*

—*My dad's in Germany. You know Germany?*

—*Nope.*

—*It's real nice. He went there, but he didn't come back yet. Where is your dad?*

The girl went quiet for a second, her fingers jabbing intently at the screen a few times before she replied:

—*Dad died.*

—*Died?*

—*Yep. Died.*

—*And he didn't come back?*

The girl considered for a moment, then left the cell phone and looked up at her grandma.

—*No, he didn't come back. Right, Grandma?*

The grandmother was silent for a long while, then gave a few involuntary gasps. *That's right*, she said finally, her voice trembling, *he didn't come back yet*, her tone disbelieving, as if she had only now discovered this.

Tears rolled down the old woman's cheeks; she cried silently at first, then began to sob out loud, and when the passengers turned to look, the young woman had her arms around the older woman, and was tenderly rubbing her back.

THE NOOSE BOY

REMOVE UNWANTED HAIR FOR *good with the newest laser technology.* I read the billboard on the side of the bus shelter and kept walking, anxious eyes fixed on the end of the street, past the billboard and the broken bench inside the shelter, the pale expanse of the model's armpit printed on my mind until it was dislodged by the headlights of the bus, which appeared in the distance on the opposite side of the street, beeping its horn and sending a near-hysterical thrill through the group of waiting people, who thronged toward it.

I should have got here two minutes earlier, I thought, cursing my luck, knowing that I was certainly not going to enjoy the luxury of sitting on a seat in the bus, and I'd be lucky to even find somewhere to stand. *Might as well try.* As I stepped into the road to cross to the other side I suddenly saw the rope dangling in the air, and before I knew what was happening, I could feel the cold touch of the braid under my chin and grazing my face, and I squealed in terror and stepped backward, dodging the noose, and heard the mocking laugh.

I looked up toward the source of the laugh, and there I saw him, a boy of fifteen or so with a malevolent face, lying on his stomach on top of the bus shelter. *Goddamn you,* I screamed in fury, taking hold of the thick rope so as to pull it from him, but at the same moment he yanked it toward him, so that it flayed the palm of my hand, and dissolved into laughter again. *You psycho!* I shrieked, my voice trembling, and he responded with an obscenity. Two women standing nearby asked if I was okay, and one handed me a tissue; nobody else looked like they were planning to intervene. With my hands clasped to my neck, I crossed the road, my heart pounding violently, but by that point the bus had pulled away, and I was going to have to wait for a miracle to send me another one.

On the other side, I stood and watched the boy with a mixture of fear and hatred, pressing the tissue against the friction burn in my palm; twenty minutes went by and he was still there, his slight frame and the darkness keeping him out of sight, lying in wait like a sly marksman, with only his head peering out. When a lone woman approached, he'd skillfully let down the noose, and although I was too far away to hear anything, I could guess that he was answering the screams and insults with the same malicious laugh.

After that I stopped paying attention, because I was doing sums in my head as I listened to the constant cries of *Jaramana, Jaramana, leaving right now, Jaramana* from the drivers of the shared taxis lined up near the bus stop, resolving to ignore them once I'd worked out I really couldn't afford the fare. *I'll wait for the bus*, I told myself, then responded to a phone call from a journalist who asked a few questions for a report he was writing about the workshop on "strengthening citizenship," organized by a humanitarian organization based in the capital, which I'd just that day attended, and after that I called my husband to let him know I'd be late, and since it was nearly nine p.m. I spoke to my son too, reminding him to check his timetable and put the right books in his rucksack ready for school the next day and wishing him good night, and then just as I'd hung up, I spotted the headlights of the bus, and at the very same moment I heard the scream.

You little wretch! On the opposite side, a man had the boy by the arm and was yelling this over and over as he shoved him to the ground and began to punch and kick him.

Either curiosity or a vengeful urge or a mix of the two made me ignore the bus and cross the street to join the other bystanders and watch: the wife of the man was hovering to one side, one hand fearfully clutching at her neck, while her husband, still punching and kicking, furiously recounted to the circle of people how he'd stopped to buy cigarettes from the kiosk, his wife a few paces in front of him, when he heard her shriek and saw the rope and the boy; the men listened intently, some occasionally contributing a kick or a punch or an insult of their own, but the boy himself was guffawing brazenly in a way that only increased the man's rage and violence, and then brazen became witless, and in a few moments more he was wailing bitterly. *Leave him now, that's enough, for the Prophet's sake*, cried the man's wife, tugging at his elbow, so he gave the boy one last kick in the stomach for luck, then left him, a sniveling, groaning, trembling heap on the ground, and walked away huffing and puffing with his wife.

A young man standing among the observers stepped forward to help the boy, who gripped the extended arm and leapt to his feet, baring a face streaked with blood and tears and snot. *They hanged my mother*, he yelped brokenly, eyes fixed on the young man. *They hanged her.*

There is no power or strength but in God! exclaimed the young man, and I heard the same words murmured by other voices around me. Who were "they"? How had they hanged her? And why? Nobody dared ask; we just looked fearfully at one another as the cold crept into our bodies, a cold I knew well, a harsh cold that made the bones hurt and the heart shudder.

A woman held out a small plastic bottle of water to the boy as he stood leaning on the young man's arm, and he poured the water down his throat in one go, then loosed himself from the arm and tossed the bottle aside, wiped the snot and blood from his nose with the palm of his hand, glancing left and right, dragged his feet with difficulty to where the rope lay on the ground and threw it over one shoulder, turned his back to go, and then suddenly looked back toward us, spat in our direction, burst out laughing, clambered up the side of the bus shelter, and lay down on the roof with his rope.

an excerpt from

DESERTION

a novel by SOMAR SHEHADEH

translated by ELISABETH JAQUETTE

WHEN JOURIE LEARNED HER brother Abdullah would soon be on leave from the military and coming home, she wanted to go to Hanano Street to get the Homs-style sweets he liked, the kind they used to devour in high school. As she passed the Armenian church and turned onto Maysloun Street, she thought about how happy Abdullah would be when he tasted them. She wanted to make him happy.

But later that evening, when Abdullah came out of the bathroom and headed to the living room, where the family had prepared a feast in his honor, and saw Jourie exiting the kitchen to surprise him with the sweets, he looked at her with a mix of shock and pity she couldn't understand. Their father, mother Zeinab, and baby brother Marwan followed Abdullah to the table, where their sister Afraa was already waiting. To Jourie, Abdullah looked like he was eating just to please the family, who had missed their son and didn't quite know how to celebrate him. Marwan sat next to his older brother, eating patiently and trying his best to behave.

Afraa pointed out her naughty little brother's unusual manners and laughed. Zeinab pushed more food in front of Abdullah, encouraging him to eat, and when she tried again their father shot her a look. "Abdullah isn't a child, let him eat in peace," he said.

Abdullah's silence surprised Jourie; she was waiting for him to say how much he loved her and had missed her. She gazed at the sweets she had bought and worried when she caught her brother's eye. What a glare! Why? Because she wanted to make him happy? She looked at the sweets at the end of the long table and realized they were out of reach; she couldn't nudge one in front of him so he could taste something from childhood. Distraught, she stood up to leave.

Abdullah glanced at her, and their eyes met without emotion. He didn't ask her to stay, didn't appear concerned that she was getting up. No one cared that she was leaving. She went to her bedroom and inside, leaning against the closed door, she took a deep breath that ended in tears. What had happened to Abdullah this time? What new terrible things were building up inside her dear brother? Had one of his fellow recruits died? Had Abdullah buried him with his own hands? No one in the house had asked him about his service as an ambulance driver.

They all assumed that this young man, who had been so sensitive his entire life, must have seen things too horrible to utter. So he remained silent; how could young men fighting in a war they opposed explain their heroism or defeats? Jourie knew how fragile and sensitive Abdullah was. She remembered when he had joined the army years earlier. He hadn't waited to finish his studies in Tishreen University's Science Department; in summer 2010, well before the war, he submitted an urgent request to enlist. He wanted to get his mandatory service over with and start his life! Compulsory military service had long been an obstacle between young men and the rest of their lives. Their father opposed the decision, their mother cried because it would take him away from them, and even Jourie, who empathized with his rush, thought the decision a hasty one.

Now Abdullah was home on leave after his first tour, and even if at first Jourie and their mother didn't know exactly what pained him, they would soon understand. Abdullah gave their mother his military field jacket to wash and left the house. She was saddened by his behavior; he wasn't spending time with her or treating her like a son should. He was her eldest son, and they had always been close. She cursed the law that snatched up young men and tossed them into the jaws of torture and humiliation; that was what must be weighing on her son. But as she looked through the pockets of his jacket before washing it, checking for anything he might have forgotten, she discovered the thing that had broken her son's spirit and set him adrift. There were several letters in his inner jacket pocket. Her voice cracked when she called her daughter over. Jourie came right away, and it didn't take them long to piece together why Abdullah was acting so distant. Over the course of two letters, a girl named Reem wrote how she longed for him and thought of him every night, how she understood the sacrifice he had made when he submitted his urgent request to enlist, all to hasten the arrival of the day when they could meet under the same roof: that was the day she was waiting for, hoping for, and dreaming of in her lonely nights. After the kisses, longing, hugs, and promises to wait for him for all of eternity, she signed the letter with a heart followed by her first name. It was dated just two weeks after he had enlisted. Zeinab pushed the letter away, shaking at having discovered her son's secret. So this was why he had joined the army before finishing his studies, why he had refused to explain his strange decision—unjustifiable except by love, and clearly against this girl's wishes.

In her second letter, Reem asked how Abdullah was doing, and told him she read the letter delivered by an assistant in the infantry school. In his letter, he asked her if the yellow wax he used to seal it was intact when it arrived; if so, they could trust their messenger. She reassured him the wax hadn't been touched and said this antiquated gesture had made her laugh.

Jourie's interest was piqued by one letter in particular; it had been ripped into little pieces and folded up. She put the scraps of paper on the ground and sat down next to it, putting it back together so she could read what it said. The words of love and longing had apparently faded. Reem's tone was more dry and to the point: she asked how he was doing and then told him she couldn't go on like this. She was tired of waiting for tomorrow and could no longer stand her family's insistence that she marry the man they had chosen for her; they knew nothing about Abdullah or his place in her life. Then she turned the blame on him, saying he should have asked for her hand before his service began.

Jourie looked up from the letter—"That slut! What a bitch!"—and her tongue unleashed a flurry of curses that would have shocked her mother had she overheard. Jourie knew that this girl had hurt Abdullah, and she stood up, wiping her tears and raising her palms to the sky.

Jourie found another letter written in her brother's handwriting in which he told his beloved, the light of his eyes, how much he missed her. He described his terrible sleepless nights, the sun that roasted their asses all day as they stood on the asphalt, and the stenches he no longer found offensive: filthy beds, filthy toilets, filthy clothes, filthy people, this filthy country... Jourie tried to hold back her tears at the painful opening to a letter he never sent. He wrote how pure his love for her was, that she gave him the strength to face any challenge. Instead of blaming her, he expressed the full extent of his love for her. He wrote that whenever they shouted in his face, whenever they cursed at him, whenever he and his fellow recruits were punished collectively, he imagined her: he thought about her eyes, hands, and hair, he thought about her waiting for him, he forgot every insult… and he ended the letter by asking her to wait for him, and not to take his will to live.

Later that day, as Jourie was about to leave for university, Abdullah returned looking tired and dejected. Their mother rushed to check on him. "I went out for a walk and got tired," he told her. "The sea air in Latakia isn't good for me, it's too humid here. I'll feel better tomorrow when I get to my post in al-Nabek, near Damascus. It's drier inland."

Abdullah went out the following day, still brooding. Zeinab and Jourie were silent too; they knew why he was sad but felt powerless to intervene. Jourie pulled a blanket over herself to ward off the cold and thought about her brother, building a new image of him in her mind. Their relationship had changed over the past several years, and now they hardly knew each other. That's why she felt so lonely at home. She summoned memories of their first family vacation, a long time ago now, and the first time he collapsed.

"Was he having difficulty breathing?" the doctor on call at the hospital had asked.

"No," their mother had replied quickly. "He was just emotional."

Her husband had looked at her in surprise, and she had stopped herself. Telling the doctor that her son was emotional meant nothing; it was no more than a mother's anxious explanation for her son's symptoms.

That evening, Jourie sat next to Abdullah in the room overlooking their neighborhood of Qalaa, watching him suffer as if from low blood pressure or anemia. "You look like someone broke your heart!" she said, trying to encourage him to share what was ailing him. Then she laughed and went on. "Is that what's going on? If so, just say the word and I'll help you win her back, or I'll find someone prettier and better. You sit tight and let me help."

But Abdullah paid her no attention. Instead, he sat there dully and strangely lumpish, as if he had decided to distance himself from this life that was bringing him so much pain. Pain of being left by someone he'd changed the course of his life for, pain of the humiliation he endured in military training.

As Jourie was looking for warmth and trying to nod off, she thought to herself that the cruelest part of love was the waiting: not waiting to be reunited with a lover, but waiting to get over having lost them. There was no point in saying "time heals all wounds." Cruelty was indelible. And if a person couldn't respond with greater, more powerful cruelty of their own, they would crumble. They'd find themself without happiness, without desire, and without the life they'd dreamed of, instead watching like a helpless bystander as that life faded into the distance.

But even though he seemed so miserable, a small part of her envied him.

His sadness seemed noble, tantalizing somehow, and she found herself wishing for something like it, hoping one day to experience the kind of love that could cause such despair. Could it only be found in a lover's lonely sorrow?

Abdullah wandered through the house. He watched Zeinab tidy up various bags, and watched Jourie help her with the same determination he had observed in her since she was young. He looked over at Afraa and saw her gazing out at the horizon. He looked at Marwan and saw the epitome of good behavior. He glanced around for their father, and saw him sitting in the living room, looking broken and preoccupied. Abdullah's gaze moved among the members of the family, and he realized it wasn't that they were avoiding looking at him, it was that they didn't see him. He let out a loud guffaw. Everyone turned to look at him. A tear traced its way down his mother's cheek. Jourie gave him a tender, understanding smile. "There is no power or strength except by God," his father intoned.

Abdullah entered the kitchen and walked over to the window. He looked at the empty ghee cans in which his mother had planted flowers, then out the window at the street, across the street at the city, and across the city at his family's fate. He loved Latakia, loved going out on the streets and saying hello to people. He left the kitchen and was heading to the front door when Marwan saw him and ran to tell their father. Their father stood up, called Abdullah's name, and ran after his son, who had by then opened the door and was partway down the stairs. Abdullah wondered at his father, at this strange man following him, descending each step as if trying to crush it under his feet. He decided to wait for the strange man and tell him exactly how fed up he was with all his shouting and the brusque way he moved.

Abdullah waited for the strange man to reach him, stood there waiting for him, and when the man finally reached him, Abdullah tried to resist. But the man grabbed hold of him and dragged him back to that strange house, where a strange family gathered around him, helping the strange man tie him up. Once they were certain he was secure, they began to discuss his fate. Shocked and subdued, Abdullah grasped that they planned to take him to a village far from Latakia. He didn't consider objecting to what they were doing. Instead, he gazed at the empty ghee cans that this woman called Zeinab was using as flowerpots. As the strangers and their commotion surrounded him, he thought to himself that he needed a ghee can like one of those, to grow wild carnations.

He seemed calmer, so the man loosened the rope and asked his eldest daughter to lock the door. Then they all went to their rooms, except for the woman Zeinab, who stayed and glanced over at him intermittently throughout the night. He tried to call out to her, tried to say her name—Zeinab—tried to catch her eye, hoping she would sympathize with him. He stared at her, waiting for her to bend down and untie the rope binding his hands.

Jourie came out of her room and saw Zeinab standing there, looking at her son. They gestured at each other and then untied him.

Abdullah stood up, and with head down he nudged his mother into the kitchen, toward the window, and pointed at the ghee cans. She didn't understand. He opened the window, thrust his hands into the darkness outside, pulled a flowerpot through the metal window grate, and placed it in front of her. He felt like she understood. She looked through the odds and ends under the sink and pulled out an empty ghee can. He took it in his hands with laughing eyes and joy in his heart. He stepped close to Zeinab, this empathetic woman, and placed his lips on her forehead. She felt a kind of happiness she had not experienced in years. Abdullah walked away holding the can and sat down happily on the living room sofa. Zeinab stood there gazing at her son, and then went to bed as the hours advanced toward dawn.

Abdullah wandered around the house holding the ghee can, stopping in front of window after window, filled with irrepressible delight. Marwan came out of his room to go to the bathroom and tried to avoid his brother. Abdullah turned toward Marwan as if to give him a hug, but the boy fled from his path. Later, Jourie got up and went to the kitchen and found her brother standing by the front door, empty ghee can in his hands, waiting for someone to open the door. She stopped behind him and made a sound, and he turned around and stared at her with a bewitched, pleading gaze. Confused, she stepped closer and went to touch her brother's hand, but he shrunk away from her. She started back toward her room, but he just stood there, waiting for her, that pleading gaze turning to tears on his bright face. She couldn't resist his pleading. She motioned him aside: here she was now. She walked over to the door, inserted the key, unlocked it, and was about to open the door for him when to her surprise he pushed her out of the way.

Jourie was standing just a few steps from her brother; his eyes filled with gratitude and reassurance, and she reached out to make him stay, but he ran off holding the ghee can, lightly descending the stairs and running out into the street. Jourie knew she hadn't made a mistake; she was helping Abdullah survive. She also knew she would wait until morning to wake her father and tell him his son had run away, and she knew she wouldn't lie; she would say, just as her mother would, that she couldn't resist his pleading gaze.

In the early hours of dawn, Abdullah sat on a marble bench in the corner of al-Nour Mosque in the Qalaa neighborhood of Latakia, thinking about the family he had left behind and how happy he felt bounding down the stairs. The silent streets mesmerized him, the ghee can's wild carnations stayed with him, and a chilly breeze stung his hands, eyes, and cheeks. The city of Latakia was revealed before him as he sat in the mosque. Through the far-off dawn light he caught a glimpse of the sea, and he thought of the sixty-six steps he'd climbed to reach this marble bench and greet the city. He reached into the can and used his finger to lift the lid, which the woman in that strange house hadn't fully removed. With his finger, he pried the lid all the way out of the can, and with a desperate gaze and passion in his heart, he used it to slice through the veins of his left hand. Wild carnations poured from his imagination and ran through his blood. They streamed through the streets of Latakia, until he let his head rest on the garden wall of the National Museum and passed out.

THE VISIT
PART 2

by FADWA AL-ABBOUD

translated by MAISAA TANJOUR

THEY BROUGHT HIM ALONG with his weapon; he would not stay silent or rest. He frightened the new residents and made the old ones laugh, instilling terror in the visitors who heard his screams all the time. No one visits him. They placed him next to me; our shoulders almost touching, yet a line of ants and earthworms separated us.

He talks to silent people, or perhaps figments of his imagination. He shouts at them relentlessly, sometimes imploringly, and at other times requesting their forgiveness. Occasionally he hurls obscene insults at them, asking them to say something instead of just staring at him and at this *whore*—and, of course, he doesn't mean me; rather, he refers to the one sprouting from his shoulder like a malignant tumor, causing inflammation.

In his rare moments of serenity, he cracks jokes reminiscent of those made by the lonely or soldiers on the front lines. He tells me about his sweetheart, who abandoned him for a wealthy man, and about his mother confined to a wheelchair. Amid his episodes of panic, he shares stories of torment, of people who lied to him and deceived him into believing he would be saved from all of this. Occasionally, he cries bitterly, questioning the elderly couple about a tree and a river, as he has been hungry for what feels like an eternity and thirsty for even longer.

The elderly pair, however, meet him with silence.

The guard, too—who ascends the hill every evening for a beer and conversation with us, praising our camaraderie, our ability to keep secrets and listen attentively without interruption—has taken to locking the door of his room, leaving the light on, and rarely making an appearance since this most recent guest arrived and transformed the place into a madhouse.

He rises at night and staggers through the darkness, swaying from right to left, inadvertently stepping on the shoulder of a child or a woman. This earns him a stinging curse directed at his parents, his family, and the day they brought him there and here.

He crosses the fence, traversing the dirt path. He throws the weapon away and hurries back, as if wolves were closing in on him. He shouts joyfully that he succeeded this time. However, as soon as he arrives, it reappears over his shoulder.

Meanwhile, the old woman shouts at the angel, "Record my actions, you fool, and why did our Father in heaven give you these two wings? To shake the moths off the walls!"

Our problem here is how to pass the time between two visits, how to cope with our yearning, or how to infiltrate the lives of those we love without alarming them. But his real dilemma lies in how to rid himself of that thing in his hand, and every attempt to discard it is met with its reappearance. Each day, after midnight, he crosses the fence and the tree-lined path, pursued by the howls of distant dogs as he tries to dispose of it. He throws it away and returns, yet that thing emerges in his hand again, prompting him to scream and curse.

I tell him that profanities here do not solve the problem, and he should do what I did: *accept the situation.*

I learned that from the old couple who left recently. Their remains were relocated to another place, but their advice helped me endure the long days and loneliness of nights.

He says he has seen me before, but I believe it's just another delusion, or perhaps it's because I'm the only one willing to talk to him. Most people here know him, and they hide their children—with crushed skulls—from him, asking him to stay away from their path.

In his scarce moments of tranquillity, he confides in me that he didn't like doing those things, but they persuaded him, they deceived him. He lowers his voice as he whispers in a tone heavy with shame, "They tempted me with money."

Every night he gets up, drags himself laboriously, stumbles more than once, ventures further than the previous night, throws it away, only to return and find it awaiting him. Lately, his obsession is finding fresh water, a beautiful caring woman, and trees that talk (someone convinced him of this).

The guard passed by carrying a bucket of water. He quenched everyone's thirst except his; he left him parched.

I don't know why the wise here don't advise him to do something, and I don't know where his guardian angel is; there is one that accompanies each of us.

The elderly pair said, "Killers are born with hollow shoulders. Otherwise, how could the shoulder carry the killing tool and the angel together?"

They fell silent suddenly when they saw him, and refused to turn toward him. None of those who promised to remember him paid a visit.

He seems lonely and thirsty; I will try to sneak into Laure's dream, hoping that she might visit us and quench his thirst and mine. This seems like betrayal on my part, but I pity him.

Yesterday evening, angry individuals came, vandalized his tombstone, and wrote: *Here lies a killer.*

It was as though he didn't recognize himself.

He felt astonished and began to repeat, "But my name was different there." He tried to recall it and asked me to help him remember, but I couldn't. He said that if he remembered that word, perhaps he might get rid of the one written on the marble. His name was stuck in his mouth, and as soon as he uttered it, a crow flew in front of his face.

He tried a lot, and then he cried.

This morning, Laure visited me. He was sitting next to me when she arrived carrying a bunch of flowers. She cleaned the weeds and thorns and planted the new flowers. She was gone for two minutes and came back carrying a bucket of water. Then she watered both of us together. I know Laure; she is the daughter of my heart. She saw the dryness of his throat, so she watered him until his thirst was quenched.

When she got up, he burst into tears. Then he asked me to forgive him.

"For what?" I asked.

He started to contort in pain.

"Never mind," I reassured him, calming his fear.

Laure approached, and a sudden tremor passed through him. "I remember her," he said. "This girl was the last person I laid eyes on."

Then he continued, "I aimed at her head. Directly toward her head; I don't know how the woman's body appeared and how the bullet penetrated the woman's head instead of hers."

He paused and then added sadly, "You were my last victim; after that I died."

EXISTENTIAL TURMOIL

by FADWA AL-ABBOUD

translated by ELISABETH JAQUETTE

HANDS IN YOUR COAT pockets, you're thinking about writing.

You're here because the bullet missed you and hit someone else. You both happened to be walking down the same street, but he preceded you en route to death. You remember his errant gaze, and how he quickened his pace toward nothingness.

Watch his body on the edge of death: his twitching feet, the light being snuffed from his eyes. Consider how similar death is to the moment you wake, unexpectedly, from a blissful trance.

You're thinking about rearranging the letters of the alphabet. Like building blocks scattered then reassembled; are you really thinking about a new skateboard? Are you thinking about salvation through writing?

The wind tousles the ends of your short hair. You watch the thread of blood, you follow its course, all the way to Cain and Abel: one a prisoner, the other waiting to conceal his crimes. A small crow sits in a tree nearby.

Crow watches.

Crow calls: *caw... caw.*

Crow teaches you about burial.

I'm not the killer, Crow. I'm the third side in the triangle of death, the holy trinity: killer—victim—survivor.

You stare at his heavenly eyes and their dull gaze. He could have been your lover, your child, or a passing fling. Here he is, completing his final and necessary task.

You keep walking, leaving the body behind.

His eyes follow you, boring holes into your back.

Are you there?

Once, you closed your eyes for a moment and your father appeared—angry, as usual—punching the wall and shouting, "If these walls could talk!"

Who am I to command the walls to speak?

You trace handprints on the wall, spatterings of blood, bullets and marks on the ground resulting from the killing. (The wall, the victim.)

It could have been you standing there with your face to the wall and your back to the killer, waiting for the Angel of Death with his gray eyes. You step closer and stand like a prisoner, hands bound behind your back, forehead pressed to the wall.

Someone walks by and stares at you curiously.

What's wrong with that woman? asks someone else.

The corpse rolls over and stares at you with pure and final tenderness. You think about the moment of panic that crossed his eyes, about bullets etching shame on victims' backs, about the broken words of their final soliloquy.

(Time does not reverse itself after each death.)

You bear the shame of existence because the bullet missed you. Now here you are among the survivors.

In the moment between when the trigger was pulled and death, did you feel a sense of panic, or surrender? Or nothingness...

You think about his shuddering heart and dry throat. You think about the victim's eyes.

Here you are. But the killer doesn't see you, even as he aims his bullets at your spine.

The victim stares into your eyes, he wants to tell you one last thing. Don't be afraid, here he is as he once was, "a dream or an idea."

(A dream in the mind of a young woman, an ordinary man resurrected today.)

Here he comes, translucent as light itself. He'll need time to learn the secret channels into his friends' dreams. He'll frighten them with brief visits to the worlds of their slumber, and be frightened himself by their alarm. The dead wander behind your door, tugging at the curtains, the younger ones blowing out candles, the older ones asking for their due: write about us.

Who am I to make words cry?

Here he is, preparing for death, fearfully watching your eyes.

Who was he thinking about before he died?

Why didn't he turn toward his killer?

Why did he surrender his face to the wall?

Why didn't he look into the eyes of his killer one last time? (The killer who would turn him into a memory.)

Here you are, aiming your soul and your heart at the wall.

What have you to say, O wall?

(I've been miserable in this country: first a place to piss on, then a space for scrawled obscenities, and finally a killing field.)

You think of all the books you've read, how you're holding on to these moments of terror, how you grip them tight and refuse to go mad.

You carry your personal failings and shame, those you've borne since you were young. Now, you must keep walking and maintain your composure, as if nothing happened.

Now, you'll open the locks and consider your failings and shame.

(Your personal failings, which were only practice for the greater ones.)

THE COWARD

a play by OMAR AL JBAAI

translated by MAISAA TANJOUR

CAST OF CHARACTERS:[1]

SAADO: In his mid-thirties.

RADEEF: In his mid-thirties.

(*A kitchen. SAADO stands at the center, hands resting on his waist. In one hand, he holds a lighter, and in the other, a metal stovetop kettle. He closely examines the gas stove.*

Profound silence disturbed by the irregular drips from the water tap.

---

1. It is possible for the two characters to be presented as women; in such a scenario, adjustments to the text and characters would be necessary.

SAADO thinks for a long time, then approaches the gas stove. He places the kettle over a burner and attempts to turn the knob, but fails to do so. Trying another burner yields the same result. He brings the lighter closer to the burner, but to no avail.

SAADO returns to stand in the center of the kitchen, scrutinizing the stove intently. Eventually, an idea occurs to him while staring at the kettle. He moves toward it and makes another futile attempt to turn the knob. He lifts the kettle. Frustration sets in as he places it back, trying the knob once more without success. Transferring the kettle to a different burner, his nervous attempt goes awry as his hand slips, causing the kettle to tumble to the ground with a resounding clang; water spills.)

SAADO (*fuming*): Screw that motherfucker[2] who created you. (*The initial outburst of words quickly morphs into an unintelligible whisper.*)

(*RADEEF walks into the kitchen, bare-chested and looking as if he has just woken up or hasn't slept in ages. Surveying the scene, he understands the situation.*)

RADEEF (*ready to go back to his room*): I thought something happened to Fustuk.

---

2. If this sentence may pose issues for the audience, it can be replaced with unintelligible insults or a similar alternative.

SAADO: What's wrong with this goddam stove?

(*RADEEF heads to the stove, turns one of its knobs, and a flame ignites on one of the burners.*)

RADEEF (*turning the knob off*): Nothing.

SAADO (*surprised*): How come?

(*SAADO, in his turn, approaches the stove and attempts, unsuccessfully, to ignite one of the burners.*)

RADEEF: Push in and turn.

(*SAADO does as instructed and one of the burners ignites. He repeats the process a few more times, as if he were the first to discover fire.*)

SAADO (*refilling the kettle*): Oh, the wonders of technology!

RADEEF (*as he exits*): Seriously, NASA material right there!

SAADO: Isn't Fustuk in your room?

RADEEF: I don't know, I'll check now.

(*RADEEF leaves. SAADO ignites the burner and places the kettle on it. He fiddles with the other three knobs, gazing at the stove admiringly.*)

SAADO (*muttering to himself*): By God, why all this complexity? It's just a knob.

(*A brief silence.*)

RADEEF (*heard from a distance as he moves away from the kitchen*): Maybe to reduce suicide rates!

(*SAADO freezes for a little while, halting his fiddling with the knobs. He stares carefully at the stove. Silence. Bringing his nose closer to a burner, he mimics turning a knob with his hand, taking a sniff. Silence punctuated by the sound of water dripping. SAADO straightens up, making his way to the countertop, where the yerba maté[3] set is. Without bothering to wash the used cup, he empties it of the old leaves and refills it from the yerba container. The persistent sound of dripping water, coupled with the wait for the kettle to heat up, starts to unnerve him, leading to a fleeting loss of composure. He approaches the sink, attempting to tighten the tap handle, but the dripping continues. Blocking the water with his finger, complete silence prevails for the first time. As the water in the kettle heats up, SAADO grabs it. The drip sound resumes. SAADO pours the hot water into a thermos flask, then from the thermos into his yerba maté. Lighting a cigarette, he heads back to the tap, carrying both the maté*

---

3.   Yerba maté: a South American herbal beverage prepared in a gourd or cup (or simply maté) and drunk through a metal or wood straw (bombilla). It has also become popular in the Levant, especially in Syria and Lebanon.

and cigarette. Placing the cup on the countertop, he once again stops the dripping with his finger. The drip sound subsides. SAADO tries to reach for the maté with the hand that holds his cigarette. After several attempts, he successfully grasps it,[4] *indulging in a sip followed by a draw on his cigarette. Leaning against the sink, he now balances the maté and cigarette in one hand, while the other continues to block the tap spout behind him. He takes a puff on his cigarette and slurps the maté through the bombilla. A brief silence, shattered by the explosive rupture of a water tank, unleashing a colossal wave. SAADO swiftly raises his hand to shield his cigarette from extinguishing, yet he succumbs to the oncoming flood. We see nothing on the stage but a sea of water, with SAADO's hand raised high, clutching the cigarette and maté. Before long, SAADO's head emerges from beneath the water. He takes a sip of maté, puffs on the cigarette, and then sinks again. The water recedes as suddenly as it surged, and SAADO reappears, standing exactly where he was with his back against the sink, one hand still reaching back to plug the tap spout. The only noticeable change is his lifted hand holding the maté and cigarette. RADEEF enters, briefly glances at SAADO, and then ambles indifferently toward the dish rack.)*

RADEEF (*starts making instant coffee*): Why are you raising your hand?

---

4. Saado's attempts can be choreographed as a dance or full-fledged pantomime scene.

SAADO (*noticing and lowering his hand*): I'm not raising it.

(*SAADO cautiously observes RADEEF as he prepares the coffee. RADEEF reaches for the thermos to pour hot water into his coffee, but SAADO rapidly seizes it. A silent, intense struggle ensues as each attempts to wrest the thermos from the other, culminating in RADEEF's victory. He pours water into his coffee, stirs it to mix the contents, and while doing so, he intentionally makes annoying noises, clinking the spoon against the cup in a celebratory manner. RADEEF finishes stirring and walks to the sink to wash the spoon. SAADO snatches the cup, slurping the ready-made coffee with feigned delight. He then moves to the sink, standing next to RADEEF, and deliberately pours the coffee down the drain. A brief silence prevails. RADEEF then walks toward the thermos, grabs it, and returns to stand beside SAADO, slowly pouring the water into the sink. Unable to find anything else to pour, SAADO, in retaliation, lifts RADEEF, places him in the sink, and turns on the water.*)

RADEEF: The passport! Watch out for the passport, you animal.

(*SAADO quickly turns off the tap, and RADEEF produces a passport from one of his pockets. SAADO eagerly takes it and flips through its pages.*)

SAADO (*while attempting to dry the wet papers*): Why the hell is the passport with you, idiot?

RADEEF: You put it there.

(*SAADO continues drying the pages, while RADEEF sits back in the sink. Silence.*)

RADEEF: Shit on you and the thermos.

SAADO (*hangs the passport on the dish rack*): This is what you're good at (*mimicking RADEEF's words*). As for you appreciating the effort of others, never.

RADEEF: What effort, arsehole?

SAADO: See, you don't even acknowledge the effort of others. Filling the kettle and starting this spacecraft (*pointing to the stove*), waiting for the water to heat up, filling the thermos with hot water, just so that in the end, you come to waste half of it to drink this piss you call coffee. Time hangs heavy; the mere effort required for waiting is enough to lift a barge, yet you dare to question this effort.

RADEEF: Aha, so "the others *is* you"?

SAADO: Others *are*. (*RADEEF looks at him wondering.*)

(*Silence. RADEEF sits, head down, hugging knees to chest. SAADO lights a cigarette. They both seem lost in thought, reminiscing about*

*grammar lessons perhaps... childhood certainly. SAADO refills the
kettle and places it on the stove.)*

RADEEF: Am I staying seated here?

*(SAADO, watching the kettle while leaning his back against the
counter, nods. Silence.)*

RADEEF: What a great birthday party!

SAADO: Whose birthday?

RADEEF: Mine! It's today.

SAADO: Does anyone celebrate losing a year of their life?

RADEEF: Do you have a theory about that too?

SAADO: It's not my theory; it's a very old fact. Sophocles, for
example, talked about it two thousand and five hundred years
ago. Imagine that.

RADEEF: Blimey! Sophocles spoke about it two thousand and
five hundred years ago!

SAADO: Imagine.

RADEEF: Who is Sophocles?

SAADO: He's a Hellenic playwright... Greek, that is.

RADEEF: And he spoke about my birthday?

SAADO: Of course, the Hellenes had nothing else to talk about but you.

RADEEF: What did he say about my birthday?

SAADO (*begins his next statement with fixed, mummy-like facial features, but they gradually become fully animated*): Sophocles had a play entitled *Aias*, or *Ajax*, depending on which language you're translating from, and Aias...

RADEEF: Or Ajax...

SAADO: Or Ajax, is a Greek hero from the Trojan War. He had a dispute with another Greek hero named Odysseus, who could also be Ulysses, Ulixes, or...

RADEEF (*interrupting*): Long story short...

SAADO: Aye, they argued about the shield of a third Greek hero, named Achilles, and the shield...

RADEEF: How many heroes did Greece have?

SAADO: Achilles is a special hero because he's a demigod. Legend has it that numerous arrows shattered against his shield. Achilles's shield at that time was like a bulletproof vest today, but imagine having only one vest in the whole world.

RADEEF: It would be with the American president.

SAADO: Man, you have a remarkable knack for screwing any conversation or anything anyone might say. *Imagine.* I said, *imagine.* It's absolutely unreasonable, really not sensible.

RADEEF: I'm sorry! What happened to Achilles's shield? Who took it in the end?

SAADO: The American president took it.

RADEEF: Where?

SAADO: To the Greek Security Council.

RADEEF (*as if saying, "Don't make fun of me."*): Come on, seriously?

SAADO: He placed the shield before the leaders of the Greek

Security Council and asked, "To whom should we grant the shield? Odysseus or Aias?"

RADEEF (*automatically*): Ajax.

SAADO: The Greek leaders favored Odysseus, though in truth, Aias was the more deserving hero, or at least Aias believed that. Especially since, practically speaking, without him, the Greeks wouldn't have been victorious over the Trojans. Feeling overlooked, Aias decides to kill the Greek leaders. He's perfectly capable of doing it, but the gods blind his heart. Instead of entering the tent where the leaders are gathered, the gods guide him to the sheep pen. There, he draws his sword and starts killing the sheep, mistakenly thinking they are the leaders. When he's done, he regains consciousness. Aye, by thy life, what a great disgrace! A hero on a hill of sheep. It's a scandal. He contemplates taking his own life, but one of his female Trojan captives says, "No, please, it's a phase, and it shall pass. There's still a whole life ahead of you." He replies, "What is this sad life that increases and decreases with every passing day?" Every day adds a day to life and subtracts a day from it. What a sentence, man.

RADEEF: Look, your kettle is boiling.

(*SAADO rushes to turn off the stove, grabs the kettle and pours the hot water into the thermos.*)

RADEEF: Honestly, I didn't feel that there was anything particularly profound in the story.

(*SAADO looks at him disapprovingly.*)

RADEEF: Yeah, it's amusing, but dig deeper into it. For example, since Aias is a hero, explore the concept of heroism. Are Aias and Achilles, along with the Greek leaders who set Troy on fire, and even the supposed defenders of Troy, heroes or criminals? Just a thought.

SAADO (*refilling his maté*): First, when I called them heroes, I meant in the dramatic sense, the protagonists, not my personal opinion. Second, if you think your talk is deep, you could be wrong; it's more depressing than deep.

RADEEF (*irritably*): You're confusing my arse. I say it's my birthday, and you hit me with "What is this life that increases and decreases with every passing day?" I bring up leaders as criminals, and you brush it off as depressing. Come on, let's dig into the concept of heroism—but nah, you mean dramatic protagonists. It's my birthday today, *Bani Adam*,[5] don't you get it?

---

5. Bani Adam: Sons of Adam or human beings, colloquially used in its plural form when addressing an individual.

(*A brief silence.*)

SAADO: The leaders are criminals!

(*Silence.*)

RADEEF: Greek leaders.

RADEEF (*after a silent interval*): And the American president who brought them the shield.

(*A brief silence.*)

RADEEF: Consider this: Change the story from a classic text written two or three thousand years ago into a narrative about today. Break down the active forces at play, their contexts, and their relationships at that time. Understand and try to apply them to our lives and power conflicts in the modern world.

(*Silence.*)

SAADO (*suddenly*): A group of sheep got into Aias's sword.

RADEEF: Or Ajax.

SAADO (*continuing, as if RADEEF doesn't exist at all*): That very sword is the one that will slay Aias. A prophecy. A maiden.

Blood. The leaders' plane brims with the dark matter and cunning of Odysseus. Odysseus, you insatiable Ulysses, have you finished devouring our building and my flesh? Is it I, or Joyce imbibing with Dubliners on the Concorde? The supersonic plane silenced the voice of Aias. Here stands his sword erect, an imperial sun beside the shining corpse of Yukio Mishima. Is today an augmentation of life or a deduction from it? Quantum physics does not answer this festering question. Did Aias perish today? Or did he, today, attain eternity? Let Aias decease as his nameless sheep did in the annals. Let us die, for the sheep in our records bear no name. Let us perish nameless, like sheep without names.

(*Applause. SAADO slowly bows in acknowledgment of the audience, and of RADEEF, who stands applauding in the sink. SAADO refills the maté and lights another cigarette, while RADEEF continues to clap.*)

SAADO: Did you really like it that much?

RADEEF (*sitting back down*): No, just being polite.

SAADO: Not a fan?

RADEEF: Frankly, it's weak and jumbled up.

SAADO: Come on! This is one of Heiner Müller's most renowned texts.

(*RADEEF stops applauding. A brief silence.*)

RADEEF: Who brought up the text? I'm talking about your performance.

SAADO: Well, that's how the text is.

RADEEF: Quite the opposite, the text is well-structured, with a language that's both poetic and harsh. It carries multiple meanings in... um...[6] (*SAADO lets him struggle for the right words.*)

SAADO: So, you really believed it's by Heiner Müller, huh?

(*Silence.*)

RADEEF: How did we even get to Heiner Müller?

SAADO: Müller, weak, the ongoing course of our lives, Aias, Sophocles, who celebrates the loss of a year of life, the passport...

(*Silence.*)

---

6. Radeef speaks spontaneously, avoiding vulgarity or magniloquence, whether discussing culture or any other topic. His sentences may vary, but he maintains a natural delivery.

RADEEF: Why don't you write a play about passports?

SAADO: To say what?

RADEEF: I don't know, I just feel like this topic is more relatable to people, about people, resembling people—people like me, regular folks, not people like you.

SAADO: What should I say? That we're suffocated? That a few stamps on the passport can dictate the trajectory and destiny of a life? That a minor embossing on the first page of the passport is considered more significant than your entire existence as a human being?[7]

RADEEF: Maybe.

SAADO: And who would bother attending, people with the embossing on the first page, or those without passports?

RADEEF: Anyone who wants to can attend.

SAADO: The president of the Republic and those in his inner circle think they're too important to grace a theater with their presence. The British ambassador, the European Commission

---

7. Saado never uses the expression *Bani Adam*.

ambassador, and the director of the Immigration and Passports Department don't bother to show up. None of those responsible for the disaster bothers to come… By God, when we put on a play, it feels like we're just talking to ourselves. You tire yourself out running from one embassy to a cultural center to the Ministry of the Interior, hoping that this play might see the light. Instead, the security clearance or visa is denied. Imagine that. Why? Because I'm deemed a threat to the state, to the national security of society, and to all servants of God. Imagine! The ambassador, the minister of the interior, and all the relevant authorities—they hold the power, the weapons, and the money, yet I am considered the one posing a danger to the state. Can you imagine that?

(*Silence.*)

RADEEF: Make me a cup of coffee.

SAADO: You get down and make it.

RADEEF: I can't, it's not the right time for me to get down now.

(*SAADO begins preparing coffee for Radeef.*)

RADEEF: That's the law for you.

(*SAADO looks at him, questioning.*)

RADEEF: They have the power, money, and weapons by law. It's their job, just as theater is yours.

SAADO: Authority, money, and weapons kill, but theater does not.

RADEEF (*possibly hinting at SAADO*): Theater kills its creator.

(*SAADO pours hot water from his thermos into RADEEF's coffee cup and hands it to him.*)

SAADO (*slightly perturbed*): Stop being pompous.

(*RADEEF drinks his coffee, while SAADO refills his maté.*)

RADEEF: I'm just saying! Thanks (*pointing to the coffee*).

(*Silence.*)

RADEEF: You come here, brew the perfect maté, light the finest cigarette, and repeat the ritual, yet you struggle to write a play.

(*Silence.*)

RADEEF: And you want the director of Immigration and Passports Department to attend.

SAADO: Shut up.

RADEEF: And you want me to stop talking. What else do you want?

SAADO: That's enough.

RADEEF: You want to love, don't you, since you're not after casual flings? Or are you skipping the whole sex thing altogether?

SAADO (*angrily and threateningly*): Radeef.

RADEEF: You're well aware I know your taste in women like the back of my hand. Long soft hair, dewy wheat skin, a well-defined waist. I've never seen you with someone like that, but heavens, I've heard you talk about them enough times. Do you think it's because the ear falls in love before the eye, or is it because you enjoy using your tongue? (*RADEEF gestures that SAADO is only good at talking.*)

(*Grabbing RADEEF by the collar, SAADO tosses him over his shoulder like a bag of wheat or cement and strides toward the kitchen door.*)

RADEEF (*remarks as SAADO walks*): They won't let you travel, fine, but they won't let you love or step out from behind these walls either? They've triumphed over you. Imagine that. Have you ever noticed how many times you say "imagine" in a day?

(*SAADO reaches the kitchen door, throws RADEEF out, and returns anxiously to his maté and cigarette.*)

RADEEF (*by the door, unseen*): Imagine stepping out from the front door. Who the hell is Müller? Who's even heard of him, man? Go out and take Müller's daughter for a date, have a drink with him personally at...

(*While RADEEF is speaking, SAADO returns to the door and nervously slams it shut.*)

RADEEF (*in a muffled voice*): You almost cut my finger, you animal.

SAADO (*losing control of himself*): I want to smash your head too, you piece of shit... What do you know about love, huh? What do you know about me and love... What do you know about my life? When we were partying in the bars, you still couldn't tell the difference between Coke and soda, you pimp... You annoyed my arse talking about the Long Island cocktail... Did you ever try savoring the Long Island? I am the Long Island, beware.[8] When... (*He suddenly interrupts himself to imitate RADEEF.*) "Love is a tiny word, tiny. (*He stretches the last letter to suggest how small it is.*) Love is here and everywhere (*hits different parts of his body, even the knee, for example*), in the knee, oh yeah, in the knee, it fills you up..." I don't want to go out. Yes, this is the finest maté and best cigarette.

(*Silence. SAADO refills his cup and lights a cigarette, still very disturbed.*)

SAADO (*muttering to himself*): Fuck you and Müller, what's with this nonsense about having a drink with him? (*Suddenly yelling toward the door*) Müller is dead, you moron, and I don't want to have a drink with anyone. It's my life, bro, and I want to scrape it against the wall until it crumbles and fades away. You got a problem with that? I enjoy scraping, is that okay? I want to scrape it until it's worn out and wasted. Got a problem with my dick? I want to scrape it too. I'm free to do whatever I damn please... Or should I go out, experience love, have fun but then get crushed? There's nothing harder than touching beauty and then losing it... What's even tougher is seeing hope, great hope for a real life, a colorful and sweet hope like cotton candy. It gets closer,

8. A play on a notorious phrase used by Syrian mukhabarat, "We are the State, beware of crossing us."

you reach out your hand, your fingers stretch, you're almost touching it, then whoosh, it crumples right in front of your eyes, a hair's breadth away from your fingers, and you're crushed away with it, and your life falls apart. The scumbag who crushed you and squeezed the joy out of your life is living the real deal, while you're stuck at the bottom like a piece of crap on his shoe, and every step he takes grinds you down even more. Do you understand me?

(SAADO becomes aware that he is talking to himself... He falls silent. He may cry too. The sound of footsteps ascending the stairs outside interrupts the moment. SAADO freezes in place, like a trapped mouse. He stares into the void, panic creeping over his rigid gaze and stiffened body. He listens intently, not uttering a word or making a move. The footsteps halt. A knock on a door. SAADO is on the verge of collapsing. The door opens, indistinct murmurs are heard, and then the door closes. SAADO begins to relax. He becomes conscious of the lingering fear in his body, so he smiles mockingly at himself. Leaning against the sink again, he lights a cigarette and refills his maté. His gaze wanders into space, seemingly thinking of some moving image. A sudden blackout. The kitchen door swings open. RADEEF enters carrying a birthday cake with lit candles.)

RADEEF *(as he enters, starts singing)*: Happy birthday to me, happy birthday to me, happy birthday, happy birthday, happy birthday to me.

(Their laughter grows louder, and with it, the stage is bathed in a rather intense light, accompanied by lively festive music. Simultaneously, RADEEF places the cake on the kitchen countertop, yet no sound emanates from the stage now except for the cheerful music. RADEEF speaks, cheerfully explaining something to SAADO. We do not hear; we see the stage as if we are watching a silent film. As RADEEF exits, the party music blends with a prerecorded audio and concert music, until the former fades completely, leaving only the music from the recording, while the silent scene continues on the stage.)

SCENE
RADEEF *returns carrying two chairs, a tarabiza,*[9] *and a large paper bag. SAADO takes the chairs and sets them up with the tarabiza in between. Meanwhile, RADEEF takes a bottle of arak from the bag, opens it, and starts arranging some meze on the tarabiza.*
AUDIO RECORDING
Music.

---

9. Tarabiza: a small tea or coffee table.

SCENE

SAADO fetches two glasses from the dish rack, pouring a mixture of arak and water into each. Seated on the chairs, they clink glasses and share a toast. SAADO appears to recount to RADEEF the fear he experienced due to the foot-steps on the stairs. They laugh and drink another toast.

AUDIO RECORDING

SAADO'S VOICE *(music continues): Hello... hello? No, "good evening" is better, good evening... What, what? I shouldn't say "what" to a woman I'm inviting to my birth-day party! Good evening, how are you? Fine... (He laughs as if she said something to him.) By the way... (He thinks for a moment.)*

SCENE

A different, better-tuned song starts, evoking a shared history, prompting them to rise and start dancing together.

AUDIO RECORDING

Music.

SCENE

They dance.

AUDIO RECORDING

SAADO'S VOICE *(over the ongoing music): By the way, the red you're wearing looks nice... (Evaluating the statement, he seems unimpressed.) By the way, I... (exasperated) Ugh... You've been trying for six months and still haven't mustered the courage to talk to her, you little... insignificant person... six months... half a year, a hundred and who knows how many days, can you imagine? Disgusting.*

SCENE

During the dance, RADEEF takes out two ropes from the bag. He ties an adjustable noose at one of each, leaving the other end free. SAADO sizes up the two nooses, then gives a thumbs up in approval.

AUDIO RECORDING

As the music plays on, the murmurs of the guests rise. The place looks crowded, but we cannot comprehend the words. This noise, coupled with the music, serves as the backdrop for the dialogues in the audio recording.

SCENE

RADEEF retrieves two carrots from the bag and attaches each to the end of a rope. SAADO secures a noose around his waist, and RADEEF does the same. Two ropes dangle from their midsection, each ending with a carrot almost touching the ground. SAADO fetches two matchboxes, placing one in front of RADEEF's carrot, and tossing the other in front of his own. They assume a position ready for a race. The objective is to push the matchbox with the carrot to the edge of the kitchen by thrusting their waists back and forth, causing the rope and carrot to move. (There is no need to point out—or perhaps it is worth noting—that the carrot resembles a fallen penis, and the body movement during the attempt to push the matchbox with the carrot is analogous to intercourse.) They seem to count to three and then start the race. The erratic movement of the rope and carrot pushes the matchbox in different directions, potentially eliciting laughter from SAADO and RADEEF. They also attempt to prevent each other from cheating, using their feet or hands to manipulate the movement.

At some point during the game, RADEEF takes out his mobile phone and begins recording. SAADO seems reluctant, but RADEEF continues filming. SAADO pauses, loosens his noose, and then tries to throw it like a lasso to catch RADEEF's mobile phone.

AUDIO RECORDING

FEMALE VOICE: *Hasn't Sameer arrived yet?*

SAADO'S VOICE (*welcoming someone*): *Ibrahim Ibrahimovic, how are you?*

IBRAHIM'S VOICE: *Happy birthday, dear.*

MALE VOICE (*whispering to a female*): *It seems that he intends to rat him out, leaving him neither happy nor intact.*

FEMALE VOICE: *Don't worry about him... Where is Sameer?*

MALE VOICE (*to SAADO*): *You've been stuck on Solene for six months, and now you're here kissing up to Ibrahim!*

SAADO'S VOICE: *I'm waiting for the right moment.*

MALE VOICE: *Bullshit!*

SAADO'S VOICE: *Talking to her directly isn't a good idea. (To the female voice) Hasn't Sameer arrived yet?*

FEMALE VOICE (*noticing SAMEER's arrival*): *Here he is.*

SAMEER'S VOICE: *Hello.*

MALE VOICE: *Directly? For fuck's sake, it's been six months!*

SAMEER'S VOICE: *Happy birthday, Saado Khanum.*[10]

SAADO'S VOICE: *Who brought you here in the end?*

SAMEER'S VOICE: *Nah, this time I did it by myself. I was going to do it to myself, but I did it on my own.*

FEMALE VOICE: *Amazing prepositions!*

SAMEER'S VOICE: *All the way, I kept saying to myself, "Oh Abu Samra,*[11] *life is nothing but the enjoyment of vanity,*[12] *and he who fears the ghoul will encounter him." Then, comrade Ibrahim shows up.*

MALE VOICE: *What is the secret behind inviting him? (Pointing to IBRAHIM.)*

SAADO'S VOICE: *First off, if I don't invite him, he'll rat us out; you know, gatherings of more than two people are forbidden. Secondly, maybe this chick can keep quiet for once.*

FEMALE VOICE: *If my big mouth is bothering you, I can zip it and leave.*

---

10. Khanum: a Persian term for lady or madam. It is a respectful and polite way to address or refer to a woman; used playfully in this context.
11. Abu followed by a nickname is a term of endearment.
12. Qur'an, Al Imran: 185.

SAADO'S VOICE: *No, don't leave until I've talked to Solene.*

SAMEER'S VOICE: *Haven't you talked to Solene yet?*

MALE VOICE: *He only talked to Ibrahim.*

FEMALE VOICE: *I'll go and discuss the matter with her.*

SAADO'S VOICE: *No, no, I...*

EVERYONE'S VOICES: *What's the holdup? Just do it now... It's not like she's Queen Elizabeth... If it were my father, he would have spoken to her by now, man.*

SAADO'S VOICE *(annoyed): Okay, fine, I get it.*

SCENE

Subsequently, RADEEF releases his noose and throws it cow-boy-style to catch SAADO's neck. Upon succeeding, he pulls the rope to tighten the noose. SAADO appears to be suffocating. RADEEF pounces on him, placing his hands on SAADO's neck and throwing him to the ground, as if attempting to strangle him. However, SAADO rises again, objecting in a manner that suggests, "Not like this." RADEEF appears to have come up with an idea. He heads to the small table, takes his cup, hands

SAADO his own, places the table behind SAADO, and then climbs onto it. After drinking a toast, RADEEF pulls the rope, mimicking the act of hanging SAADO. Concurrently, he notices the cake with extinguished candles, hits his forehead, and leaps toward the cake. SAADO also hits his head, seemingly forgetting the cake is an important matter. He puts the table back in its place, while RADEEF adds and lights new candles on the cake.

AUDIO RECORDING

(We hear the sound of SAADO's footsteps as he approaches SOLENE.)

MALE VOICE: *Give me a cigarette.*

FEMALE VOICE *(we hear the lighter's flick): Have you finalized the dates with the gallery?*

SAMEER'S VOICE: *Oh, right, you need to stop by the printing shop to give them the measurements. What a terrible whiskey!*

MALE VOICE: *It's homemade, sir.*

FEMALE VOICE: *My beloved homeland, the greatest of homelands,*[13] *every time...*

---

13. A reference to a pan-Arab musical created in Egypt in 1960.

SCENE

RADEEF approaches SAADO with the cake. When he reaches SAADO, the recording concludes with SAADO saying "hello," and right after that, they start singing the birthday song.

AUDIO RECORDING

(The voices gradually fade away, and we hear SAADO's voice speaking to SOLENE.)

SAADO'S VOICE: *Hello...*[14]

(With the rope still around SAADO's neck and the carrot swaying with his movement, SAADO and RADEEF sing cheerfully. During the song, SAADO raises the carrot, pretending to shoot fire upward, reminiscent of wedding celebrations.)

SAADO AND RADEEF: Happy birthday to me/you, happy birthday to me/you, happy birthday, happy birthday, happy birthday to me/you.

---

14. If this script were to be staged, the production team could improvise another silent scene, evoking dualities such as life and death, sadness and joy, love and animosity, etc.

RADEEF: Blow, you blow them out (*stopping SAADO*). Wait a minute. (*He seems to be making a wish.*) Now, blow.

(*SAADO blows out the candles, keeping his hand raised in a firing gesture. Complete blackout. Silence. The stage lights up again. SAADO stands, leaning against the sink, blocking the water tap behind him with one hand, while the other is raised upward as if shooting. The kettle is on the stove. The passport is not on the dish rack. RADEEF enters, dressed elegantly.*)

RADEEF (*starts preparing instant coffee*): Why are you raising your hand?

SAADO (*lowering his hand*): I'm not raising it.

(*Noticing the kettle, SAADO moves toward it. The sound of water dripping is absent. He pours the hot water into the thermos, then from the thermos into a yerba maté cup. RADEEF, using SAADO's thermos, prepares his own coffee. While stirring, the spoon unintentionally clinks against the cup. RADEEF lights a cigarette, grabs his cup, and leans against the counter. Silence.*)

SAADO: Have you finished hanging out?

RADEEF (*looking at him*): Hanging out!

(*Silence.*)

RADEEF: How long have you been here?

SAADO: Where?

RADEEF: In the kitchen.

SAADO: I don't know, about an hour.

RADEEF: An hour!

(*Silence.*)

RADEEF: Where's Fustuk?

SAADO: Where's she?

RADEEF: I am asking you!

SAADO: Are you testing me?

RADEEF: Don't you smell something foul?

SAADO (*sniffs*): Nope.

RADEEF: You don't... and you've been here for almost an hour...

SAADO (*interrupting*): I left Fustuk snoozing on the brown chair.

RADEEF: You left her sleeping on the chair an hour ago to contemplate your next masterpiece play right here in the kitchen!

SAADO: What's with these existential questions? What's wrong with you?

RADEEF: With *me*? I went camping for three days and came back fresh as a daisy. What's wrong with the God who created you?

SAADO: *Me*? I'm twice as fresh as you.

RADEEF: You can smell the stench a mile away, you idiot. Fustuk shat everywhere, and now she's hiding under my bed. Did I ever ask you for anything in my life? This is the only time... I didn't even ask you to clean up after her, just to leave the door open so she wouldn't shit everywhere. I begged you, reminded you, and warned you, and you shook your head like a lizard. "Don't worry, your wish is my command, Fustuk is like a sister to me." You should've told me you didn't want to... you should've said no... you...

SAADO (*interrupting*): Have you not been at home for three days?

(*Silence. They look at each other.*)

RADEEF: How long have you been in the kitchen?

(*Silence.*)

SAADO: I don't know.

(*Silence.*)

RADEEF: I'll start looking for a house.

SAADO: No. (*After a brief silence*) Do you want to leave me because of a cat?

RADEEF: No, I want to leave you because this is no way to live; it's a life unfit for human consumption.

SAADO: Exactly, and you know how many times I've thought about suicide. What stopped me was your presence only. If you want to leave the house for good...

RADEEF: Great! You'll be able to commit suicide without me bothering you or you bothering me. All I asked was for you to leave the balcony door open. Is there anything easier than that? You don't want to leave the house, I get it. But a door, man, a cat (*grabbing SAADO and shaking him*). What is it called? This... inaction? Isn't it death? Isn't it suicide?

(*Silence. RADEEF maintains his grip on SAADO. SAADO reaches for his cigarette, takes a drag, then seizes the cup, sipping the maté. RADEEF releases his hold, briefly gazes at him, and exits the kitchen. SAADO seems on the edge of collapsing.*)

RADEEF (*his voice is heard from outside the kitchen*): Saado, where are your clothes?

SAADO (*wiping his eyes and steadying himself*): I burned them.

(*Silence.*)

RADEEF (*peeks his head out from behind the kitchen door, looking astounded*): You burned your clothes!?

(*SAADO nods. RADEEF's head disappears. SAADO looks perplexed, torn between thinking, drinking maté, smoking, and trying to understand RADEEF's actions. Eventually, he grabs the maté cup and smashes it against the ground... RADEEF enters, carrying a laptop and clothes.*)

RADEEF (*looking at the shattered cup*): Strip.

(*SAADO, bewildered, stares at RADEEF.*)

RADEEF: Come on.

(*SAADO begins sweeping the shattered glass directly into the dustpan, removing larger fragments. After disposing of them in the bin, he places the bombilla and remaining cup pieces back onto the tray.*)

RADEEF (*almost shouting*): Saado... Put on these clothes right now, take the laptop, and go down to write in some café, garden, or any place other than this shithole. Hurry up.

SAADO (*sweeping again*): Your clothes are too small for me.

(*Silence.*)

RADEEF (*placing the laptop on the countertop, tossing the clothes at SAADO, then snatching the broom from him as he heads toward the door*): Either you leave or I will. (*He exits.*)

(*Blackout... or lights up... or any indication signaling that the play has ended. SAADO applauds, as if encouraging the audience to join in after the performance.*)

SAADO (*clapping*): Bravo, bravo, a well-executed ending. It's either work or suicide. The duality of being or nothingness, dynamism or fixism, zero or one, black or white; dualities stretching as far as the eye can see, reducing existence to binaries. Bravo.

(*RADEEF enters, visibly surprised.*)

SAADO: Now you're like the Trojan girl who urged Aias not to end his life, insisting there's still life ahead. She encouraged him to live, not to choose suicide!

RADEEF: Who is Aias?

(*SAADO looks at him disapprovingly. Silence.*)

SAADO: Aias... Ajax?

(*RADEEF seems confused.*)

SAADO: Aias, the Greek hero who conquered the Trojans but later took his own life because he killed the sheep.

RADEEF: So, I'm a Trojan girl. What about you? A Greek hero?

SAADO: Pick up the things you've scattered around. (*He starts preparing maté again in a new cup.*) Don't confine my life to just two options.

RADEEF: Do you truly see yourself as a hero?

SAADO: Absolutely, anyone who can bear this life is a hero.

RADEEF: Fine, hero, you're saying Aias conquered the Trojans and then offed himself. What have you defeated?

(*Silence.*)

RADEEF: If I've reduced your life to two options, you're the one limiting it completely. Tomorrow, I'll start looking for a house. I know you won't commit suicide (*as he leaves*) because you're a coward.

SAADO (*pulls a knife from the dish rack*): Radeef. (*RADEEF looks at him, horrified.*) Death is easy, eternal, with no suffering, no search for meaning. Life is what requires courage, not death… and as you said, I am a coward.

(*SAADO stabs himself and falls quietly to the ground, while RADEEF stands shocked. Blackout.*)

RADEEF'S VOICE (*heard in the darkness*): Not bad, just a tad melodramatic.

SAADO'S VOICE: No, it's a tragedy; the hero's death in the end.

RADEEF'S VOICE: Maybe, but why didn't you choose writing instead of suicide?

SAADO'S VOICE: It crossed my mind that I might kill you too, or maybe both of us could leave the house. (*The lights slowly come on in the kitchen; no one is on stage, but the voices continue.*) I don't know why I leaned toward suicide.

RADEEF'S VOICE: Because it's the easier option.

SAADO'S VOICE: Maybe, but it's just as easy for you to present me with two options; the challenge is leaving the options open, much like life.

RADEEF'S VOICE: So the hardest part is to live.

SAADO'S VOICE: The toughest and yet the most beautiful.

RADEEF'S VOICE: In that case, go and talk to her.

(*Voices begin to intertwine toward the end of SAADO's next sentence.*)

SAADO'S VOICE: I'm waiting for the right moment.

(*Overlapping voices: SAADO and RADEEF singing, "Happy birthday to you." A professor's voice, "The Syriacs played a crucial role in translating Greek philosophy." A child's voice, "Grandma, what are Aristotle's five fundamentals?" SAADO's voice, "If I don't invite him, he'll rat us out." The voices of a group of males chanting a slogan while running in a steady rhythm, "One united Arab nation." SAADO's voice, "What I fear most is to fall in love with you actually." A teacher's voice, "Dramaturgy has recently become a specialized field, but in practice, the director is a dramaturge, the actor as well, and every member of the crew." RADEEF's voice, "Give me a Long Island, please. Would you like to try it?" A female voice, "Leave him alone, for God's sake. He's not involved." A detective's voice, "I want names, give me names." A voice from a children's cartoon series, like* Oscar, Ox Tales, *or* Heidi, *or music from* Tom and Jerry. *A child's voice, "Sixth grade, second division, ready to perform the flag salute, my honorable comrade." A piercing scream of pain. A female voice, "What are you expecting me to do? Kneel down and beg, 'Please don't leave me'?" Another female voice, "As if you're the political eggheads." RADEEF's voice, "You have many possibilities." SAADO's voice, "But I have no hope.")*[15]

This text was written as part of the Writing for the Stage project, supported by the Citizens/Artists Foundation. A substantial portion of the work was read at Hammana Artist House in December 2020, attended by friends and local residents.

---

15. Through this intermingling of voices, I tried to condense an entire human life. If my efforts fall short, I trust that either the production team or the reader's imagination will bring it to completion.

SPRING DIARY

by ODAI AL ZOUBI
translated by ELISABETH JAQUETTE

MY MOTHER WAS ADMITTED to the hospital yesterday, and the doctor said she won't be leaving.

Full coma.

This diary is about her.

They say writing helps: helps you overcome challenges, helps you understand yourself and the universe. Writing has helped me a lot in the past. It hasn't fixed my problems, made me more accepting, given meaning to life, or added beauty to the world. But in some not-so-insignificant way, it's helped me.

I hope it helps this time too.

*   *   *

1

My sister can't stop crying. I don't get it. They weren't close.
Maybe that's the reason she's been crying nonstop. She's
fought with Mom over everything since she boarded the boat
to Germany. She got divorced, then got back together with her
ex. Yesterday, after the doctor said what he said, she called me
at least a dozen times. Then she decided to go to Syria. Ever
since she became German and got a German passport, she's
been able to travel. My sister never would have gone back to
Syria if Mom hadn't gotten sick. She and Dad wanted me to
meet up with her in Beirut before she crossed into Syria, since
I can't enter the country myself.

I decided not to pick up the phone when they called, not
today and not tomorrow. But I couldn't go through with it.

2

Since we got the news, I've been remembering the way she was
in my childhood. When I was in elementary school, she kissed
me on the forehead every morning and night, whispering that
I was her favorite person in the whole universe. I was strug-
gling with my grades, being bullied, and my relationships
with my teachers.

She stopped when I began eighth grade, stopped kissing
me on the forehead. I'd gained self-confidence, my relationships with other students and the teachers had improved, and
I was a better student, maybe thanks to my tutors. I didn't

want her to treat me like a child. Or maybe there were no more kisses on the forehead because I'd grown taller? Or because she'd already reassured me?

Last night I woke up several times, shaking: my sister, father, wife, daughter, aunts, grandmother, grandfather, and third- and fourth-grade teachers had all kissed me on the forehead, saying I was their favorite.

But not my mom.

3

I haven't seen her since I fled Syria in late 2012, aside from three times in Beirut.

On our last visit she met my daughter for the first time. My daughter always speaks Swedish, and her Arabic is broken and hard to understand. Mom tried to play and joke around with her, even tried to tell her a bedtime story. She failed at all of it.

My daughter said this grandmother, who wears a hijab when outside the house and cooks inedible food (she doesn't like Syrian cuisine), isn't the kind of grandmother her friends in kindergarten talk about, not the kind we read about in books and see on TV.

It was disappointing for Mom, who couldn't give my daughter all the love she'd tended in her heart since my sister and I left Syria. It was frustrating for my daughter, who wanted a grandmother like the ones her friends in kindergarten had. That's normal.

In the end, they came to understand each other, a bit. But it was nothing like the pure and overpowering love I'd experienced with my grandparents, which God had granted me.

4

She was always reminiscing about her one trip to Egypt in the mid-nineties, as if it had represented the culmination of all humankind's desire for tourism and travel.

We made fun of her sometimes. We'd tell her there's more to Earth than Egypt. Unlike Mom, we'd never left Syria, but we were certain she was exaggerating. We told her about India, Japan, New York, Paris, Berlin.

But Mom wasn't convinced. She said she didn't want to visit foreign countries. She'd suffocate. Later, after the war, she said she wouldn't come see us in Germany or Sweden, even if we became European and it were easier for her to get a visa.

For Mom, Egypt was still the "Mother of the World," as the saying goes.

I told her I'd go with her to Egypt again.

We never did.

Egypt banned Syrians from entry.

5

Twice, my dad beat me violently. I cried a lot, but what made me saddest was my mom. She tentatively tried to stop him, but afterward she blamed me. "It was your mistake, your fault," she said with conviction, and a touch of sadness she herself might not have understood.

That was the first time: I was an eight-year-old child, and he beat me because he got a call from the school principal about me.

The second time I was older and didn't expect Mom to act any different. Even so, I couldn't help but wait for her to intervene somehow. At least, for her not to repeat the same words.

But she did. With the same conviction, though less sadness.

Both times she pulled me to her chest afterward, rocking me as if I were still a babe in her arms, unable to speak or stand.

6

I think I was around fifteen when I discovered her love of gossip. Mom taught us not to bad-mouth anyone, she was strict about that. But she herself used to gossip about her younger sister, my father's older sister, two of our neighbors, and anyone else less important to her. For her, talking behind someone's back was fine so long as it wasn't hurtful and you didn't spread rumors about them. That was the rule she held herself to.

She also taught us to be forgiving, even though she herself never forgave her younger sister. Mom stopped speaking to her for two years, until their father fell sick for the final time, which forced her to end the estrangement.

Mom believed she'd never bad-mouthed anyone in her life, that she had a big heart and forgave everyone.

From my mother, I inherited a love of gossip, the desire to forgive, and an aversion to causing harm.

7

Mom never believed in evolution. She has a vague faith in magic and jinns, and in heaven and hell, of course. When I tried to explain that religious symbols shouldn't be taken literally, which is what Ibn Sina and the Brethren of Purity said centuries ago, she came close to tears. And she asked me not to speak of it under her roof again.

As different as we were when it came to faith, we were quite similar on social and personal matters. For example, we both preferred the same group of relatives, and both couldn't stand another group.

In that regard, we were remarkably similar.

8

The doctor let us speak to her today. I mean, I saw her and talked to her on WhatsApp. My sister and dad were in the room with her.

My sister said Mom squeezed her hand when she heard my voice, or rather my uncontrolled sobbing.

The doctor smiled when my sister told him this and nodded somewhat skeptically.

I know that patients' families imagine all kinds of fantastical things, but my sister is sure of it.

After the call, I was overcome by an indescribable nostalgia for the two days I spent with her after having my tonsils removed. It was just us at home, and she sat next to me and sang songs by Fairuz. I was in the front row, and she squeezed my hand with unparalleled tenderness.

9

Mom and Dad changed a lot during the war years. Dad—who hadn't even cried when his own parents passed away, who was master of the house and everything in it—now cried whenever we saw each other, and even when we spoke on the phone. He cried at home when relatives or friends died too.

Mom doesn't cry anymore. She used to, when she was younger. But she hasn't cried since my sister and I left. She snaps at her family now and has a sharp tongue for her siblings and their children.

The first time we met in Beirut, Dad cried when I left. Mom said she'd never see me again. Her heart told her so, and a mother's heart was never wrong; she was sure of it. But she didn't cry.

Mom's heart was wrong.

10

Mom hasn't eaten chicken since the avian flu outbreak in the late nineties.

Eventually the epidemic faded, or maybe even ended completely. But she could never eat chicken again.

11

Mom loved the singer Warda Al-Jazairia. I listened to "Black Eyes" today, one of Mom's favorite songs. Other favorites included "In Exchange for Love," "It Feels Like Love," and "Wanderer," by her beloved Abdel Halim Hafez.

I listened closely to the lyrics as if studying them, as if reliving Mom's youth: furtively smoking like a mixed-up teenager, drinking coffee, smiling at life and the years that wrought what they did. I realized, for the first time, that the lyrics are: "Accompanied by piccolos late into the night." For decades, I'd been singing "Accompanied by people so late into the night." It's *people* who stay up late into the night with us, who make the weighty years of death, illness, and longing tolerable. It's *people* we chat, laugh, and stay up late with; *people* who stay up late with us, helping us bear the unbearable. People, Warda. People: my mother, family, and friends.

But none of those people are here. I stay up late and sing to myself.

Did Mom know the actual lyrics?

12

We tried our best to get through the war years. We avoided anything sentimental and the indecency of nostalgia. But at one point Mom had a total breakdown.

It was after her eldest sister's funeral. She called me when she got home and completely broke down. She said she couldn't keep living alone, without her children, anymore; she wanted me by her side. Life was too taxing and cruel, and it was killing her. She said my aunt sent more kisses to me and my sister than the rest of her relatives around the deathbed. She didn't want to die in Syria without us, she added. That would be unbearable, unacceptable.

It was the only time she bared everything in her heart.

13

Mom almost boycotted my sister's wedding, but in the end, she bent to social pressure.

For years my sister had been engaged to a man she met in university. Then one day she left him, explaining that she was in love with a friend of his: his closest friend, his "bestie," as they say in English.

Since I was younger than my sister, I had no say in any of this, and anyway, my life and values were starting to change. I watched the battles from a distance. I sympathized a bit with my sister and her argument, although it was simplistic and not entirely convincing: "The heart wants what it wants,

Mom. I'm not doing anything wrong," she repeated a thousand times a day.

"You've no more heart than brains," Mom snapped.

Mom worried for my sister's reputation, and for ours. I don't think she liked my sister's mercurial, fiery, and at times caustic nature, which was nothing like her own.

Mom remained apprehensive of their marriage. When they divorced, she told me it was the best thing that ever happened to my sister.

But when she got back together with her ex, Mom exploded at me. She didn't dare express what was simmering inside her to my sister.

"'The heart wants what it wants?' I swear to God, she can't be my daughter. That girl's just like her aunt…"

My sister, too, said she was nothing like Mom, as if they came from two different planets.

14

Mom asked me how I was raising my daughter, if I was going to raise her according to Islam. I hesitated before responding. I didn't know the answer.

I mean, I want our daughter to know her Muslim heritage. But my wife and I aren't practicing, and needless to say we're not going to make her abide by something we don't believe in ourselves. Mom was shocked. I was too. I thought she knew I'd given up on organized religion decades ago. But she hadn't known at all. Maybe she thought that was youthful rebellion. Maybe my mom doesn't know me as well as I'd thought.

15

She always said I'd understand when God blessed me with children.

I think she was right. Now I understand.

Now, all I want is for my daughter to live nearby for the rest of my life, to see her every weekend even after she grows up and leaves home, to know that her future is secure. For her to ask me my opinion when she makes major life decisions, and minor ones too. And somewhat paradoxically, I want her to be her own person, not a copy of me. I want her to know I'm proud of her, that I'll always be there for her. And I want to protect her from everything: from young men who would hurt her, from financial need, from other people's cruelty—racist white Europeans and ever-angry Syrians alike—from boredom, from the foolishness of youth that can be truly dangerous, from...

Now I understand that raising children is tremendously challenging and incredibly sweet, that this love is unlike anything in the universe, that it's a fact of life.

And now I understand that my hopes are futile: my daughter will live her own life, separate and independent from me. She'll rebel against us as a teenager, she'll begin to come around in her thirties. And maybe, if we're lucky, one day we'll truly be close.

So, as Mom said and Dad agreed, I'd understand when God blessed me with children.

If I hadn't been blessed with a daughter, I probably wouldn't have understood what Mom said.

On the other hand, I don't think either my sister or my mom understood the slightest thing about their own strange relationship.

16

Mom said my sister was too embarrassed to introduce her to her German friends.

My sister tried to get Mom to visit her in Germany, despite Mom's protests that she didn't want to go to Europe. At any rate, my sister didn't succeed, because the procedures for bringing family into the country make it so difficult. My sister couldn't travel to Beirut or any Arab country, because she was living in Germany as a refugee, and Arab countries don't admit refugees, not even for short trips. So, Europe was the only place where she could see Mom and Dad. I entered Europe "legally," which means I can travel to Lebanon and see family there.

While waiting to hear back on the visa application, my sister told Mom all the ways she'd need to change: she shouldn't wear her usual white veil and black coat while in Germany, and she maybe shouldn't wear a veil at all (my sister stopped wearing one two years after the war began; I had supported her, but never expected her to lash out at Mom about it one day). She shouldn't criticize my sister in front of strangers, shouldn't constantly pray for the children in a loud whisper the way she was known to do, shouldn't knock on wood to ward off the evil eye...

Mom never went to Germany, and she never understood why my sister was embarrassed by her.

17

Mom always felt for our neighbor Um Nouri, while Dad hated the woman.

Um Nouri was cheating on her husband with her cousin. We all lived in the same neighborhood, and since neighbors keep an eye on each other, our family knew about it. Um Nouri's husband, Abu Nouri, beat her and abused her in public. Dad believed Abu Nouri beat her because he suspected her of cheating on him, so it was her fault, whereas Mom believed his abuse had led to the affair, and so it was his fault. It all came out over dinner one evening, the only time something like that happened. I mean, for Mom and Dad to fight over something serious in front of us kids.

I remember Um Nouri as very beautiful, and very kind. Her son Nouri was younger than me, and just as kind. I hardly remember Abu Nouri.

The situation repeated itself with my eldest cousin. She was five years younger than my mom, and they were close.

My cousin left her husband and came to live with us for two weeks. She didn't love him and wanted a divorce. Naturally, Dad was firmly opposed to the divorce. I don't remember the details, but in the end she was victorious—she did divorce him, though with a black eye. Then she went to Dubai, remarried, and got divorced again.

Dad lorded the second divorce over Mom. Mom couldn't defend her, now in Dubai with a Portuguese boyfriend, living in sin like foreigners do. It was a resounding scandal and a black mark on the family's reputation; not even my sister and I escaped ridicule from neighbors, relatives, and friends.

When Mom said she felt for Um Nouri, Dad nearly lost it. But he was also confused by his response. He respected his wife's kind and forgiving nature. He didn't want to raise his voice at her in front of us, and barely managed to control himself at the table. He cursed Um Nouri and all the women on Earth, then got up and stormed out of the house.

Mom remained calm, smiling sadly. She said she despised Um Nouri and her lover, but the girl (Um Nouri was ten years younger than her) didn't deserve to be beaten. Beating someone, just like cheating on them, was wrong.

Then she sighed and said that life is difficult and complicated sometimes.

18

Did she love Dad?

Yes, of course. But it was a dull, traditional love.

He wasn't very attentive and, aside from a few times, was never affectionate with her—at least not in front of us. But he respected her and her role in general, never hit her or shouted at her.

My wife says that's not love, that's habit and submission. I'm not so sure.

19

On her third trip to Beirut, Mom revealed some of what had preoccupied her the night before I'd left. She took me to the Corniche so we could take a walk by ourselves. And she said what she wanted to say very quickly: shyly, tenderly, and flustered in a way she didn't try to hide.

She said she regretted having encouraged me to think for myself and regretted her pride in me at the beginning of the revolution. If I hadn't joined the revolution, I might have still been able to visit her in Syria, the way other people who had left the country could now do. She was deprived of me. And it was crueler than she could bear. After a pause, she added that I was more precious to her than country, freedom, revolution, or defense of land and religion—and then she apologized, saying she didn't want to upset me. She knew that two of my friends had been tortured to death and her nephew had been disappeared in the regime's detention centers. But she wanted me nearby.

She was silent for a moment and then went on, less anxious and more focused.

She said she was alone now, for the first time in her life. People in Syria were busy making ends meet, waiting for the electricity to come back on, or standing in line for gasoline and other such things. She lost sleep over never having reconciled with my sister and—here she paused slightly—with me. My father had changed, he was tired. Their relationship had been based on raising children and getting by. She smiled at three boys laughing noisily. "Life by the sea is beautiful," she said, getting side-tracked. "And life in Damascus is beautiful. *Was* beautiful," she corrected herself. She went on, her thoughts wandering. She said she thought about my childhood and adolescence often. I was rebellious and questioned everything. Why did she encourage me? Why didn't she try to suppress such rebellion? In reality that's what she'd wanted, she and my father, to stamp out all kinds of rebellion. They were on the same page: we should live the way everyone else did. But she couldn't. Her heart and mind took another path, and she allowed me the freedom to question things. Neither Dad, nor his family, nor hers understood the reason behind this change. She didn't either. She had encouraged me: from my early childhood onward she bought me all kinds of books, scientific and otherwise. She answered my questions as best she could, with her limited knowledge. When, as a teenager, I stopped praying and fasting, she didn't get angry or force me to. Strange. Very strange. "Now you're a great writer, a famous writer." (Mom believes I'm successful and famous, despite my insistence to the contrary.) She didn't expect me to turn out like this, to abandon my faith, traditions, and roots. But she's happy that I have a strong moral compass, and that I'm respectful of others. Maybe it's because she wasn't strict with me, she says sheepishly, with a proud smile. And then she laughs, for the first time in this strange conversation. She never could be strict with me. She wanted to be, wanted to be strict, and chart a straight path for me, the way her father and grandfather and everyone else had done, the way Dad did with us. But she couldn't, her love for me was greater than anything else...

Then she said it wasn't important, it was all just sadness and nostalgia from an old woman no one cared about.

She ended by saying she didn't know what to say, she was feeling very confused these days.

She said she didn't want me to respond. She was just getting things off her chest; it wasn't a discussion. But she needed to say it, it would have weighed on her if she hadn't. After that, we walked for a long time, chatting about my sister and dad, my wife and daughter, the sea and our neighbors, her younger sister...

20

We may not see each other again after death.

But who knows?

I wish I could believe in anything: an Abrahamic religion, Buddhism, Shintoism, a pagan African or Native American religion from before the spread of Christianity. Anything.

I want her to see me, to watch over us, for her not to exist in pure nothingness.

I'm not exactly a materialist, but at the same time I believe humans are necessarily ignorant of the metaphysical. That's the inescapable human condition. In order to believe, we must leap into the void, and that's something I've never been able to do.

I wish I could believe in anything: Sufi metaphysics, immortality of the soul, Nirvana, eternal return, even a vast underground world where people go after death—as everyone believed before Zarathustra and his discovery of heaven and hell.

Oh God, anything!

21

She never told us much about her childhood. We never asked either.

It was a very traditional childhood. Five children, father worked an office job. Her grandfather came from the poor side of a rich family in Homs and settled in Damascus in the early twentieth century. Three girls and two boys, all of whom went to university. Her younger sister was the most outgoing and beautiful, while Mom was the most level-headed. No exciting stories about her being naughty or getting in trouble.

We know my uncles took advantage of their sisters when my grandfather passed away. With my grandmother's knowledge, they took more than their share of an inheritance that was small to begin with. But Mom quickly forgave them. One of them became fairly wealthy, and Mom didn't like his wife.

Mom wanted the world to be easy, pleasant, calm. She wasn't overly concerned with life's great joys or with other people's trespasses. To her, what mattered was that we live in peace and harmony, that we are respected and loved, and that we keep our traditions alive.

There are very few photos from her childhood, and those we do have are all black and white, worn around the edges. In them, Mom appears unsmiling, or with a pale and ghostly smile.

22

The family of great apes evolved when our hominid ancestors developed a new kind of social structure. Previously, they had lived in small, close-knit communities, used fire, and cooperated in order to survive. These communities evolved into the families we know today, with two parents and their children forming a little nucleus within larger society. For various reasons, human children are the only animals that take years to be independent from their mothers.

Despite this, or because of this, family relationships are the most complex and difficult human relations to understand. Only your family shares your entire history. And only your mother remembers certain parts of your early childhood, parts you don't even remember yourself.

Millions of years of evolution, and I sit here writing a diary about my mom while watching my daughter chase a balloon: jumping in the air, tossing it high, and failing to catch it each time it falls…

23

I don't think Mom liked my wife. She would rather I had married a normal girl—that is, not a visual artist and intellectual with opinions about everything. Mom hates intellectuals with opinions and loud voices, as she often said before I was married, referring to my cousin who studied at the College of Fine Arts. But I got married after leaving Syria, so Mom had no choice but to accept it, and pray for our health, happiness, and future children.

Anyway, she tried hard to be nice to my wife, the few times they met.

My wife said Mom loved her dearly and treated her like her own daughter.

* * *

2 4

The Arab custom that resonates most with the human spirit is the three-day period of mourning. In the time of mourning, the family of the deceased finds renewed, expanded love in the people around them. It means they won't be isolated after their loved one's death, thinking about things that are useless to contemplate.

2 5

I will not light a candle, I will not wash her body, I will not scatter dirt over her.

Alone here, waiting.

My sister said tonight might be her last.

What is she thinking about now? What is she remembering, or reliving, in the coma? Her love of mulberries, which according to my grandmother always stained Mom's clothes when she was a child? Baking chocolate cake for my sister every Friday without exception, from her childhood until she was fifteen? Her grandfather, who never let anyone raise a hand against her, for reasons we do not know? Bread lines in the eighties, or after the revolution? Her trip to Egypt? The beauty mark on her face she was so proud of, the one her mother-in-law often teased her about? Morning coffee and her favorite Fairuz song, "I Loved You, and You Know What They Say About Love"?

All through my childhood she'd kiss me cheerfully, holding her cardamom-scented morning coffee, and repeat a line from the song with cautious joy, "Looks like your sweetheart forgot your date."

What is she thinking about, in the coma, on her last night?

"Looks like your sweetheart forgot your date," Mom...

26

I'm going to stop keeping this diary. It didn't help this time.

Mom died.

It's a rainy spring here.

Will I see her again?

an excerpt from

THE
KURDISH MAQAM

a novel by MAHA HASSAN
translated by SAWAD HUSSAIN

SUNDAY, MARCH 17, 2019, PARIS

A NIGHTMARE, A NIGHTMARE *is what this is!*

Valentina couldn't get those words out; her tongue might as well have been completely paralyzed. She was keenly aware that as soon as she heard herself utter those words, she'd wake up and be free of these strangers that she had encountered again and again for roughly the past two weeks. She knew that *she* was dreaming, but the problem was the others—these people who would rant at her, shove her, not believing what was happening was only a dream, a dream that they'd all soon wake up from, each returning to his or her reality, where no one knew the other.

All at once she felt cold and sweaty. She forced out, in a whisper, the enchanted words "A nightmare, a nightmare is what this is." But she failed.

The woman standing behind her in the long line jostled her, and barked in French, "Avancez-vous, madame!"

Valentina had lived this moment before. She had lived out this very scene dozens of times: it had been on repeat for the past two weeks. How had this woman forgotten that the same event had been repeating itself, with just a few slight differences?

Valentina turned around looking for the policemen who passed by the line now and again, to keep the peace. When she noticed a young woman wearing a navy uniform with POLICE emblazoned on her vest, Valentina called out, "Madame... madame..." But her voice was too weak to be heard amid the hubbub.

An elderly gentleman stood next to Valentina. Like the others he forgot that this scene had happened before, all minute details included. "Ya ibnati, don't even try, just leave it. No one will hear you. We're all damned to this line," he relayed in French laced with Arabic.

"Mais, je suis française!" Valentina protested. "Why should I have to stand here for a residence permit? I already have French citizenship."

Valentina overhead the women behind her tell another, "As if we aren't! Yet here we all are in the same line."

Valentina spun round to address the women. "But why?"

"You're joking, right?"

"No, I really want to know!"

"Keep moving, lady, keep moving. Don't pretend you haven't heard of the new law."

"Which law?"

Everyone hushed up suddenly. Silence tinged with fear mingled with the air when they heard warnings booming from the loudspeaker, "No talking while waiting. You're always under surveillance. Anyone who chats with their neighbor in line will have their application delayed, and be stuck in more lines."

The silence did Valentina much good—she was able to hear what wouldn't have been easy to in the middle of the ruckus: a familiar voice humming a tune. *I know that voice, I know that voice*, she kept telling herself.

Her face lit up and her heart contracted with joy when she saw her mother at a distance, striding through a glass door, skipping the line, advancing as if she were an important personality, an entourage in tow—Valentina couldn't make out who they were. But she knew her mother all right from her voice, her smell, from her height, despite the distance between them. "That's my mother!" she exclaimed. The others shushed her.

Valentina started humming the tune without moving her lips, shivering from the cold. Her coat had fallen off in the pushing and shoving, and she hadn't been able to pick it back up. Feet stomped over it, and it lay abandoned a few paces behind, caked in mud.

Long hours passed while the line crawled. All the while she kept hearing that song. Her mother's voice was crystal clear; she wasn't mistaken.

Valentina fished around in the large handbag on her shoulder for her small notebook. She jotted down the notes of the tune.

Valentina found herself after a long while near the glass door, where her mother had gone in a few hours before. She caught sight of her mother behind the glass, going here, going there, still singing the same song. She couldn't control her desire to call out, but her strangled voice struggled to make it out of her throat. Her tears started to fall while she shivered in the cold, dripping sweat, until her voice finally made it out and yelled, "Ani!"

Valentina woke up to that scream, which had failed to compel her mother to turn round in her dream, but thrust Valentina out of the nightmare. Her face was wet with tears, and she saw that her blanket had fallen off; her body was quaking from the cold. She turned on the light and wrapped her brown-and-yellow woolen shawl round her shoulders. With feeble steps she made her way to the bathroom. As she sat down to relieve herself, *that* song came back to her.

Valentina knew, as she hung between waking and sleeping, that she was hallucinating because of her high temperature. Who knew that song in this Parisian quarter and would be listening to it at this time of the night? *It must all be in my head*, she assured herself as she padded back to her bed. After wrapping herself up in the blanket, she glanced at the clock. Two-thirty in the morning.

The song *still* made its way to her from somewhere.

Exhausted, she began to hum the tune. Someone else might as well have been in her head dictating the notes to her. She soon fell into a deep sleep.

"No, not again!" She found herself standing in the same line. She began to scream, "Where's the police? Where's security? This can't happen every time. I'm French... FRENCH!"

Her voice didn't make it out, and no one could hear her.

A nightmare! A nightmare is what this is!

Valentina tried to repeat the words; she alone could make this stop.

But she had to wait longer, to listen to the scoffs and rebukes of those same people. She dared to ask the woman who had been so aggressive with her earlier, "But I really don't get it. Weren't we here yesterday? And the day before? Haven't we all been here before?"

The lady looked at her and replied in a voice dripping with irritation, "The *only thing* missing in this stifling heat is the hallucinations of strangers."

Valentina was bold enough to snipe, "Aren't *you* a foreigner? Why are you talking down to me?"

"Yes, I'm a foreigner... but I'm not like you. Even us foreigners aren't all the same."

The fabric of the dream twisted subtly when a handsome young man entered, saying, "Ladies, no need to fight. We're all foreigners here—we're all in the same boat."

The elderly man, the one who mixed Arabic with French, whispered, impressing upon Valentina, "Try to be calm and just do what you're told till we get inside. You're the reason things always stop midway, and we get sent back to the beginning each time."

At this, a terrifying silence washed over the place, only pierced when the following words floated out from the loudspeaker, "No talking while waiting. You're always under surveillance. Anyone who chats with their neighbor in line will have their application delayed, and be stuck in more lines."

Valentina kept quiet. She started to hum the tune that she had found scribbled in the notebook in her bag, humming without moving her lips. She found a handkerchief at the bottom of her bag, one that she hadn't seen before. She inhaled it deeply, and murmured to herself, "Saman."

Things went better this time round. Valentina actually made it inside and got to see what it looked like for the first time. She knew that these were the doors of salvation from this hell that she had been forced to endure for the past two weeks, unable to explain or detail her legal status in this country.

She found herself standing in a foyer. Facing her was an elegant room, in which sat a beautiful woman. She bore a striking resemblance to Catherine Deneuve and was surrounded by pieces of papers and a large calculator.

Valentina entered and greeted the woman, "Bonjour."

"What are you saying? What language is that, Ms. Zaza?"

"I'm not Ms. Zaza anymore, I go by Ms. LeBaron."

"What are you saying? I don't understand you, Ms. Zaza. Do you understand my questions?"

Valentina shook her head and almost cried. She was speaking French, but this woman couldn't understand her.

The woman pressed a button on her desk, and an enormous man appeared.

"Get me a translator."

"For which language?" asked the large man.

"I don't know—for whichever language she's speaking, this Ms. Zaza."

"It's French…"

"What is she mumbling on about? This day will never end. How complex this case is. There aren't any clear facts here! What language do you speak, Ms. Zaza, so I can at least get us a translator?"

Valentina knew that the woman couldn't understand what she was saying, and so when she saw her mother pass by, she ran out of the room.

"Ani!"

The enormous guard shoved her back and growled, "Where do you think you are?"

"Okay, I think I've finally got it," the woman said. "It's Kurdish. I think the word 'ani' is 'mama' in Kurdish, or maybe Turkish. How about you send me a Kurdish translator, and let's try that out."

Valentina couldn't believe what she saw moments later. The ground below here almost gave out. Here was the person who knew her best coming into the room.

"Samano," she whispered to herself.

He cast a dismissive look her way and turned to address the civil servant. "Please, make it snappy—I'm busy."

"Okay, *sir*. Please translate what this woman is saying. She understands French but responds in some other language. I can only issue her a permit if I know what she speaks. You know that the new law segregates residents based on their first language, meaning their mother tongue."

She turned to Valentina and said, "Ms. Zaza, in order for me to submit your file to my superiors, I need to confirm how good you are in your mother tongue. Can you say the following in Kurdish: I am Valentina Zaza, and I confirm that Kurdish is my first language. I, Valentina Zaza, agree to reside in France in accordance with the new law, respecting the linguistic rules of each community."

Valentina's lips curled into an O. She could say all that in French. But in Kurdish?!

Saman cackled at the look on Valentina's face. He said to

the civil servant, "Madame, you're joking. Look at her—she can barely string together a few words in Kurdish. I'm sorry, but I won't waste any more time here. Find her a different language group. She's not welcome with us."

Valentina looked at Saman, her eyes pooling. She began to hum the tune living in her head before him, hoping to gain his sympathy, to remind him of their connection.

"Yes, Valentina," he responded. "I know, you used to sing this song to me. That was a long time ago. I'm sorry, cousin, but this is the law now. You can't speak Kurdish—you're the one who turned your back on us. Do you remember now?"

The civil servant was reading the instant translation on the screen, and so she understood what Saman was saying. "Please, let's keep it professional. I just need to know where to assign Ms. Zaza."

"Not with us, Madame. The Kurdish sector rejects her."

Valentina searched frantically for the handkerchief she had found at the bottom of her bag, the one she called Saman's desmal—at least she remembered that word. But Saman did not give her the chance to pull the memento out, to tug at his heartstrings so he'd go easy on her. Instead he glared at her and left.

Valentina started to sob. "Where's the desmal? A nightmare, a nightmare is what this is!" she kept repeating.

SATURDAY, MARCH 14, 1998, ERBIL

A nightmare, a nightmare is what this is!

Françoise woke up repeating those words and swatting the air, hoping to get away from *here*, and back to reality.

"Encore ici!" she grumbled. From time to time, she'd wake up to find herself in this place that she didn't know, and couldn't recollect how she got there. The last thing she could remember was standing next to her bicycle, chatting to Eric outside the post office in the sixteenth arrondissement. She couldn't even remember making her way back home or how she suddenly left Paris, in broad daylight, and ended up here.

Françoise couldn't find the missing link between these two places and times: Paris, Saturday, eleven forty-five in the morning, fifteen minutes before the post office closed; and here—in this place whose name she didn't know. What day was it even?

Who took her from Paris? How did Eric leave her? Did someone abduct her from her home? Off the street? Or did she get into a taxi? Where did her bike go?

She felt the onset of a crippling headache and slid off the bed. She made her way to the window. "C'est un cauchemar," she repeated to herself.

She expected to see the Seine from the window of her house on New York Avenue opposite the Alma-Marceau metro station, but instead there sat a small garden outside this house, in it a woman watering plants. Françoise yelled out, "Madame! Pouvez-vous m'aider? Je suis enlevée. Appelez la police, s'il vous plait. Aidez-moi, madame, je vous supplie!"

She'd always ask for help from anyone she came across, convinced that she had been abducted.

The woman looked at her and gestured with her hands, expressing confusion.

Françoise backed away from the window and began to stare at the room she was in, trying to fathom where she was. She stood in front of the painting of the Erbil Citadel and griped, "They've even got bad taste! My Monet should be hanging there instead."

She spotted her cigarettes on the table, and sat to have a smoke, replaying the details of that fateful day—Saturday, March 14, 1998—in her head.

Ez keçim keça kurda nim

SEVEN OF CUPS

by RASHA ABBAS

translated by ELISABETH JAQUETTE

THE TOWER

IT'S NOT TRUE THE Lord acted without warning. Before sending lightning to break the tower's back, he'd tried to communicate with us by other means. Builders failed to notice what the birds were carrying to their nests. Sand. Small stones. Every day my brother and I plucked these heavy things from the nests in the garden. Clouded mirrors and rotten wheat. Even when we paid attention to such signs, we didn't hurry to please the Lord. We were proud of the tower, proud of its existence among us. We were believers first and foremost, awaiting the moment it would enter the heart of the sky. We felt reassured that the Lord's mills were slowly grinding away. We sighed in relief at the end of winter, because we figured he would wreak his vengeance on a rainy day. But he chose a day in summer. Lightning descended, and as the tower crumbled, I ran through the valley amid falling ash and stone, outpacing the wounded who collapsed all around me. I slid into the first hole I found and stayed there until it was over. Afterward, I went out and searched the pockets of those who died above. Their stories belonged to me now, and I walk by the Lord's will. We're not heroes, we just drag the wounded to safety in times of crisis. We don't bear arms, we're not prophets or knights. Our pact with the Lord is that we don't seek glory or pay its price. He takes care of us, and we walk between the burning flames, heads bowed with the shame of our cowardice. He'll place his hands on our faces and fill our pockets with figs. We'll tell tales and guard the gates to the temple of stories. We'll memorize them and recite our pact with him, and anyone who refuses will be lost.

THE WHEEL OF FORTUNE

Twenty-four.

Twenty-two.

Both times I said a number aloud, the white ball rolled across the roulette wheel and came to rest perfectly on the number. My friend pulled me by the arm more squarely in front of the table. He asked me to put the ball back and think of the next winning number for him to bet on. It didn't work, obviously. There's an unwritten rule that a gift will vanish the minute you flaunt it, the moment you try to use it to kill someone or win their heart. It was the first time I'd tried it out in a casino. I didn't want to overuse it. Maybe my grandfather passed his gambler's genes on to me, skipping over my mother, who never touched a card in her life. Three times he lost everything he owned on that green table. With the same enthusiasm that he squandered his life at the roulette table, he joined the project of Arab Unity. He happily gave up his military rank for diplomatic work. Sitting down for breakfast one day with his family in Venezuela, the telephone rings. News of the separation, and the fall of the republic, passes through the telephone wires.

JUDGMENT

When the Judgment card appears, there's a possibility that someone from the past may suddenly emerge. A phone call will be his chosen means of reconnecting with you.

"There's no reason for you to stay in Bonn," the man on the other end of the line says. "I looked through your file myself, and it's not dangerous to return to Syria. If I were in your shoes, I'd come back as soon as possible. Your place is here, not running away in Germany without a future."

THE CHARIOT

Marta insists on two things: tarot cards never fail, and neither do signs. I don't have the energy to argue over things like this. I force myself to listen to her constant chatter, just like I force myself to endure her eccentric diet when I eat at home. I had nowhere else to go in Berlin. It took me time to understand what every box in the kitchen contained, all the alternative ingredients unfamiliar to me. Pink Himalayan salt and natural vanilla flakes, both ultimately disappointing. I'd expected them to be preferable to wood chips, in both taste and appearance. Bitter cacao beans, chia seeds. Marta had traveled to Nice early that morning. She left a note on the refrigerator informing me it was my turn to clean the bathroom and asking me to think about giving the tarot cards another chance. Maybe they could help me locate other details in my grandfather's story. The only thing I took from her note was that I was free to eat "real food" that day and wouldn't be punished by Marta's healthy cooking.

As I made my way home holding a bag that contained a burger, food which would ordinarily be banned from entering the house, my hunger and the heat made me think about how bad my situation was. The fact that I was broke, my inability to make progress with my research. I told myself it was a good time to try what Marta had been nagging me about. I told the Lord that I wanted a sign. Just two steps later, as I neared the door of Marta's building, I saw two dogs running at me until their owner yanked them back by the leash. He smiled at me. He seemed to have a physical condition that caused him to tremble. I quickly went up the stairs and unlocked the door: two dogs—on which card in Marta's deck had I seen two dogs?

I went into the laundry room that Marta had turned into her office. She'd stretched clothing lines across the room and used wooden clothespins to hang research papers and notes she wanted to review, along with a few tarot cards. I carefully inspected each card suspended there. I found the Moon card, which showed two dogs barking at the moon between two towers. There wasn't sign a more direct than that. I had a feeling that could be explained only by someone like Marta, a sense that despite this card's clear connection with the sign, it wasn't meant for me. I understood the feeling later on, when another card hanging on the line caught my eye: the Chariot. I took the card from the line, with its drawing of a cart driven by a pair of sphinx-like creatures. I sent Marta a text asking when she was coming back. I heard her phone beep somewhere in the room. It wasn't unlike her to forget or lose track of her phone. I threw myself on the couch and stared at the Chariot card, searching for any detail that might tell me something, until I fell asleep, the card still in my hand.

THE FIVE OF SWORDS

People don't like seeing swords when they're reading tarot cards. They're often an ominous set of cards: departure, a broken heart, conflict, or death. In tarot, swords symbolize the power of words or thoughts. Of the four creatures surrounding the woman on the World card, who represents creation, the sword most suits the eagle hovering in the upper right corner.

In terms of time, swords are weeks. So the Five of Swords usually means something will happen within five weeks. That's the same amount of time from when my grandfather received the call to when he made up his mind to travel back to Syria and explore the situation, a predictably dangerous move for a gambler like him.

Take a look at the palm of your hands, at a clock on the wall, or any sentence written around you. Look at it for a few seconds, glance away, and then look at it again. These are basic techniques to escape a bad dream. If the lines of the object begin to blur when you stare at it, your mind will realize you're dreaming, and you'll easily be able to escape. This is why, when my grandfather arrived in Damascus and saw two men get out of a military Jeep and head toward him, as soon as he emerged from the airport, he allowed himself a moment before he felt afraid. He looked at a round clock face outside the airport. Quarter past three in the afternoon. He stared at the clock in order to steal a glance at the two men approaching. They wore plainclothes. Lightweight brown suits and unofficial-looking shirts. The lines of the clock weren't blurred when he glanced at it again, despite the heat and the look of the Jeep, sitting there waiting for him.

As a former military officer, he had never imagined he would be driven in a car like the ones that used to mobilize at his command. One of the men reached out for a handshake with bravado. The man asked him, courteously, to accompany them. It was clear this was the best thing for him to do, to preserve what remained of his dignity. He walked to the car with the men voluntarily. The second man seemed visibly reluctant, as if he had been forced into the mission. When my grandfather sat down in the car, he thought about how easily he had been led into this trap, returning from West Germany, where he had chosen to flee. In a few moments he would enter the heart of hell, where he would remain for six months. He went back to staring at the young man. The man had a friendly manner, and when he realized he was being looked at, he turned his head away in shame. My grandfather thought he recognized the man's face from one of the reserve training courses in Aleppo he had supervised as a lieutenant colonel in the army, at the beginning of the Era of Unity. He managed to look at his palm, calmly, careful not to make any sudden erratic movements that would attract the men's attention. The lines on his palm did not blur, not even after a few seconds. Neither did the features of the young man's face when he looked away and then back again. It was not possible that this was a dream. Quite the opposite: the lines of the scene were becoming clearer, including the rise and fall of the road as they headed toward the neighborhood of al-Mizzeh. Where the famous prison stands.

an excerpt from

YESTERDAY'S ENCOUNTER

a play by MOHAMMAD AL ATTAR

translated by KATHARINE HALLS

CAST OF CHARACTERS

WALID SALEM: *Early sixties. Former major in the Syrian intelligence services. Physically fit and healthy, he looks younger than he is. Defected in late 2012 and fled to Jordan by arrangement with the Syrian opposition, then moved to Berlin with his family in early 2014 with the assistance of the German authorities. His wife died of a chronic health condition shortly afterward, and he is raising his daughter, Maha, alone.*

MAHA: *Twenty-two. Walid's daughter. Studies law at Humboldt University. Arrived in Germany at age thirteen.*

ANAS: *Forty. Came from Syria to Germany as a refugee in early 2015. Quickly learned to speak good German in Berlin and is known as an ambitious and energetic aspiring journalist and writer. People who know him describe him as sociable, but he always keeps some distance from his friends, making it difficult to really know him.*

NADIA: *Thirty-nine. Lawyer. Born in Germany to a Syrian father, and a German mother. Has made a name for herself in Berlin representing immigrants facing deportation.*

BASEL: *Thirty-nine. Left Syria and ended up in Germany in 2015 by way of a visa to pursue graduate studies in computer science. Talented in his field, he has found plenty of rewarding work opportunities in Berlin. Met Nadia, the lawyer, at a party; the pair were immediately attracted to one another and started a relationship. Has always made it clear that he wants to avoid the Syrian community in Berlin and prefers not to talk about Syria.*

THOMAS: *Sixty-five. Lawyer and member of a European human rights organization. Thomas came out of retirement after hearing Anas's story and decided that he would take on the case. He is known for his charismatic presence, understated elegance, and a good sense of humor that can emerge at even the tensest of moments.*

The events of the play take place in Berlin, between summer 2022 and spring 2023.

SYNOPSIS

ANAS encounters WALID SALEM by coincidence at Bauhaus, a home improvement store, in Berlin in summer 2022. He recognizes the man's voice; he's never seen his face. It is the voice of the man who supervised a violent interrogation of ANAS—who was blindfolded—when he was arrested in Damascus over ten years ago. Though both men thought they had begun a new chapter when they arrived in Germany, this chance encounter will change the course of their lives. ANAS seeks out THOMAS, a lawyer, who prepares a legal complaint against WALID SALEM, alleging that he was directly responsible for abuses including torture and murder. WALID SALEM is arrested by the German police as a result. He was released on bail and remains under surveillance. Other victims and witnesses join ANAS and THOMAS in their efforts to see WALID SALEM prosecuted; meanwhile, the latter—who denies all accusations against him—hires NADIA as his lawyer.

In the following scenes, THOMAS meets with his client ANAS in preparation for a much-anticipated court hearing; likewise, NADIA meets with WALID SALEM, accompanied by his daughter MAHA, who translates for him. NADIA's partner BASEL opposes her decision to represent WALID SALEM, and the disagreement strains their relationship to a breaking point.

Can a case be built on memories of events that happened over ten years ago in a place nobody can visit now? Who is telling the truth? And is there one truth?

PROLOGUE

ANAS (*addressing THOMAS, who sits on a chair facing him*):
Walid Salem.

(*Silence.*)

ANAS: His voice is engraved in my mind. I won't forget it.
Not in ten years, not in a hundred years. Even if I wanted to
forget, do you think I could? When I heard him talking on
the phone, I knew it was him.

(*Silence.*)

ANAS: Like a knife in the stomach.

SCENE 5

SETTING: *Side by side on stage, we see THOMAS meeting with
ANAS in his office, and NADIA meeting WALID SALEM and
MAHA in her office. When NADIA, WALID, and MAHA are
talking, MAHA interprets between German and Arabic. To represent
this process, it is sometimes NADIA who poses questions to WALID,
and sometimes MAHA; meanwhile, sometimes MAHA, rather than
WALID, is the one to respond to NADIA. At times, MAHA picks
up from where either NADIA or WALID has left off. At other times,
she steps outside of her interpreter role, and speaks as herself.*

THOMAS: Describe to me the first time you heard the voice of Major Walid Salem.

ANAS: It was my third day in the branch. I'd been dumped in an overcrowded cell. Two guards pulled me out and into the corridor. They blindfolded me and beat me and insulted me. Then one of them started dragging me somewhere. I could hear the screams of other people being tortured in the corridor. We went up some stairs. I heard him knocking on a door, then we entered a room, and he saluted and addressed the person in the room as "sir." The person told him to make me kneel on the floor, and then said to me: "Head down, you animal."

THOMAS: Walid Salem?

ANAS: Yes.

THOMAS: What do you remember most from that meeting with Walid Salem?

ANAS: There's one thing he said that I'll never forget. "If you don't cooperate with us, you'll never see the sun again." By that point I'd been in the cell three days, and I'd seen hell, but that was the moment when fear swallowed me up.

. . . .

NADIA: I like the Homs accent because it's my father's accent. I'm embarrassed my Arabic isn't very good. But I can understand the dialect better than standard Arabic.

WALID: Well, I'm embarrassed my German isn't better.

MAHA: Never mind, that's what I'm here for.

. . . .

THOMAS: You said you could sometimes see out from below the blindfold, if they hadn't tied it properly. Could you see Walid Salem at all? Any distinguishing features?

ANAS: Not during the interrogation. The blindfold was very tight, and anyway I had to keep my head bowed the whole time.

. . . .

NADIA: Did you recognize Anas Jaber when you saw him in Bauhaus?

WALID: No. Honestly. You have to bear in mind there were dozens of detainees coming in every day, sometimes hundreds. There's no way I'd be able to remember them all. It's been more than ten years. He's changed. When I was arrested, they showed me a photo of him and gave me some more information, and then I remembered a few details.

MAHA (*taking over*): What I remember clearly is that I recommended he be released. During the interrogation, I tried to reassure him as best I could. I even told the guards to be respectful with him, give him some tea to drink, let him smoke. I know you're probably thinking, "Why's that such a big deal?" but you have to take my word for it—that sort of thing was very important. You have a detainee who doesn't know where he is or what's going to happen to him, and the biggest thing you can do is try to make them feel safe, even if it's only relative. That's what I was trying to do, as far as possible, within the parameters of the situation. I don't know why he's denying this and saying I was the one responsible for him being tortured.

NADIA: Other plaintiffs have joined the case, so it's not just Anas Jaber that's making that accusation.

WALID (*gesturing to a weedy-looking plant next to NADIA's desk*): Tell her it needs to be repotted with some better soil.

MAHA: My father's a real plant lover. He's saying you should repot this plant.

NADIA: Oh, thanks. Honestly, I'm terrible with plants. They're always dying on me.

MAHA: In Syria we say that people like my dad are "green-fingered." Everything they touch stays alive.

. . . .

THOMAS: I'd like you to try to describe to me the inside of the intelligence services branch in as much detail as possible. The corridors, the different stories of the building, the distances between the different cells where you were taken, the torture rooms. And most importantly, Walid Salem's office in relation to all of these. I'd like you to try to draw a picture for me.

(*THOMAS hands ANAS a large blank sheet of paper.*)

ANAS: Can you explain why?

THOMAS: When Walid Salem was arrested and held in custody, he made a couple of claims in his statement. He denied that he was involved in torturing detainees; he also denied giving any kind of order, direct or indirect, that detainees should be tortured after he'd interrogated them. I'd like to show that the torture rooms were in close proximity to his office. In addition to your testimony, there's now a series of testimonies from other former detainees, and they're consistent on this point. They also say they heard the sounds of people screaming as a result of being tortured. This conclusively disproves Walid Salem's claim that he did not know they were tortured after leaving his office. It establishes that the torture was an integral part of the interrogation. That they used a good cop, bad cop approach. He never got involved; the dirty work happened before and after his part. While you're drawing, remember: Walid Salem may have deprived you of your sight, but you have your ears. You can use them to rebuild a great many details—probably more than you think.

(*ANAS begins to draw a floor plan of the building as he remembers it. A rudimentary sketch of WALID SALEM gradually appears on the backdrop as the scene proceeds.*)

. . . .

MAHA: The detainees had to be blindfolded during the interrogation so that they wouldn't recognize the interrogators if they saw them afterward?

WALID: That was the rule. I didn't make it.

MAHA: And you didn't have the authority to ask them to remove the blindfolds from the detainees while you interrogated them?

WALID: It wasn't a question of my authority. I wasn't always the only one conducting the interrogations. Even if I was the highest rank present, I couldn't necessarily trust the officers who were there with me. They could report me if I did anything suspicious during the interrogation. That did actually happen. Within the intelligence services, everyone was watching and being watched. Nobody was allowed to have a sense of absolute authority or impunity.

MAHA: So in short, there's no way Anas Jaber would be able to recognize you unless he heard your voice? Is that right?

WALID: That's right.

. . . .

ANAS: I'd be lying on my front with my legs bent, feet pointing upward. With every question or answer they'd beat the soles of my feet, my heels, my legs. I'd have to keep my legs raised, otherwise they'd beat me harder and beat me on my back too. The beating was so hard my feet would bleed. The walk back to the cell was excruciating.

THOMAS: What were you beaten with? Could you say who was beating you?

ANAS: Sometimes with a thick cable, sometimes a chain. But I couldn't say who it was.

THOMAS: Could it potentially have been Walid?

ANAS: I doubt it. His voice came from in front of me, close to my head, which was on the ground. And the beating was on my feet, coming from behind.

. . . .

MAHA: Did you subject Anas Jaber to any form of physical violence during the interrogation?

WALID: No.

MAHA: What state was he in when you saw him?

WALID: How do you mean?

MAHA: I mean, was he physically well? Or was he injured? Exhausted? Agitated? Conscious, unconscious? Aware of where he was?

WALID: The detainees were usually in a state of intense fear and anxiety. They'd usually have been beaten up before they were brought in. So it would depend on the circumstances of their arrest.

MAHA: Okay. So do you remember anything specific about Anas Jaber's physical or psychological state at the time he was brought to you?

WALID: As far as I can recall, there was nothing unusual about the state he was in.

MAHA: Meaning, he was in an ordinary physical and psychological state?

WALID: I'm not sure what "ordinary" means to you.

MAHA: He hadn't been tortured, he wasn't completely checked out, he wasn't delirious...

WALID: Well, he'd certainly been beaten. I have to stress again, that was a basic part of the arrest. But I don't remember him being in an unusually poor physical state. I don't think I'm qualified to comment on his psychological state. But no, he wasn't delirious. In general, the interrogations didn't last very long. As I've told you, interrogations at that point were a formality. Detainees were brought to me as part of the routine procedures that were followed with every case.

MAHA: So you did not use physical or psychological violence during the interrogation of Anas Jaber that took place in your office.

WALID: Correct.

MAHA: Okay. Did you ever see anyone being beaten in front of you? Even if it wasn't you who'd given the orders?

WALID: Sometimes I had to.

MAHA: Can you explain?

WALID: When they'd bring the detainees in, I'd see them beating them. Some of them were in a very bad state.

MAHA: Did you ever take part in beating them?

WALID: Sometimes I had to.

MAHA: Please explain.

WALID: As I told you, the branch chief was suspicious of me. There were times when I had to take part to allay his suspicions.

MAHA: So are we talking about torture?

WALID: No. We're talking about giving the detainee a beating, in passing, when they were being transferred to the branch chief. I had to play the part, like I said.

MAHA: Tell me a bit more about these incidents. How did you beat the detainees, or pretend to beat them?

WALID: You'd slap them, punch them, kick them... I was careful not to hurt them.

MAHA: You didn't use any implements?

WALID: No.

MAHA: Were there implements for torture?

WALID: That wasn't my area of authority.

MAHA: But you knew about them.

WALID: Like what?

MAHA: Canes, chains, whips, implements for pulling out fingernails, implements for administering electric shocks, the German chair...

. . . .

THOMAS: Why was it called the German chair?

ANAS: There's this story that a Stasi officer showed the Syrian intelligence how to use it. There's another story that some Nazis fled to Syria after the war and were allowed to stay on the condition they share their expertise with the intelligence services. Honestly, I have no idea what the real story is. Anyway, as far as I understand, it's a metal chair frame which the detainee is tied to. Then they can adjust the chair in such a way that it causes intense pain to the back and neck. If they do it hard enough it can break the spine.

THOMAS: Did you ever see it?

ANAS: No, thank God. I saw enough. But I heard about it. The stories would make your hair turn white.

. . . .

NADIA: An article came out recently, after you were arrested. (*She waves a piece of paper.*) A journalist interviewed an anonymous former detainee, who said that after you'd interrogated him, he was taken for a torture session in which false confessions were extracted. He referred to the method of torture as "al-shabih."

. . . .

ANAS: They fastened my wrists to chains suspended from the ceiling, then pulled them upward, so that I was just standing, on my tiptoes. The pain was indescribable. Just when I thought my wrists and shoulders were about to break, they'd let the chains down. Then they'd entertain themselves by beating me with a cane, all over my body.

THOMAS: Did you hear Walid Salem's voice, or were you aware of his presence, while this was taking place?

ANAS: No.

. . . .

NADIA: Did you ever give orders for a detainee to be tortured, even if you weren't the one to oversee the torture?

WALID: No.

NADIA: Never?

(*WALID shakes his head.*)

NADIA: You're sure?

WALID: Yes.

(*Silence.*)

WALID: That doesn't mean that some weren't beaten after they'd been brought to me. But not on my orders. I have to stress again that beatings were an ordinary practice within the jail. The detainees were beaten at random.

MAHA: My question about torture taking place on your orders—did that happen?

WALID: No.

. . . .

THOMAS: Did you ever see detainees who were dead?

ANAS: I saw detainees who were about to die.

. . . .

NADIA: There were detainees who died within the building, correct?

MAHA: Unfortunately.

NADIA: How?

MAHA: How did they die?

NADIA: Yes. As a direct result of torture? From illness or hunger? Or a combination?

. . . .

THOMAS: Let me put it more precisely. Did you ever see the bodies of detainees who had died within the branch?

ANAS: I saw people who were dying, and I heard people dying.

THOMAS: Did you ever see, with your own eyes, a person who was dead?

ANAS: I saw people begging to die.

THOMAS: Yes or no.

ANAS: I'm not sure.

. . . .

MAHA: I didn't have the authority to do anything. Mostly they'd already be in a terrible state when they arrived at the branch, and they'd die within days. They'd be all skin and bones, and often they'd have infected wounds. I'd try to get the worst cases transferred to hospital, but sometimes the request would be denied, and sometimes I'd be afraid they'd notice

I was trying to help the detainees. The numbers were going up, especially in late 2011. Some would beg to be allowed to die. At the end of 2012, before I defected, there was a huge number of bodies coming out of the branch each day. It felt more like a morgue. (*Switches to speaking as herself.*) I'm sorry, I need some fresh air.

NADIA: Sure. We need to wrap up for the day, anyway.

WALID: What's wrong?

MAHA: This is the first time you've talked about any of this in front of me. I feel sick just from the description. How could you bear to see all this?

WALID (*leans toward MAHA, puts his arm around her, and kisses her head*): I'm sorry you have to hear all these details.

. . . .

THOMAS: Tell me about your last interrogation with Walid.

ANAS: It was two days before I was released. I was in solitary. They took me out, but they didn't blindfold me properly. They took me to a room, and I could see electrical wires, chains, and metal prongs. I'm pretty sure they let me see on purpose, to scare me. Then they started beating me, all over my body, until I lost consciousness from the pain. I don't know how much time passed. When I came round, they dragged me to Walid Salem's office. This time they blindfolded me properly, and they made me lie face down on the floor. I distinctly remember him saying, "You gave us a hard time, huh? So we had to give you a hard time too." Then he asked me, "Do you believe his Excellency the President is capable of steering the country to safety?" I was terrified. I thought it was a trap. If I praised the president they'd know I was lying, but I couldn't say what I really thought. So I said, "I hope so."

THOMAS: What did he say?

ANAS: Nothing. He asked me if I wanted anything. I was feeling brave and asked for a cigarette. He told them to give me a cigarette and some tea. And then when they took me out, before they sent me back to solitary, they sat me down in the corridor. One of the guards said, "Looks like you've got some friends, you faggot. Have a cigarette. How many sugars?" I was too scared to say anything. He got annoyed and asked again. "I said, how many sugars?" I said, "As many as you want." He brought me a cup of tea like sugar syrup. (*Laughs nervously.*) It was like eating a tray of kunafah after fasting for a month.

THOMAS: Now you come to mention it, shall we go for dinner? I'm getting hungry.

ANAS: You know what the most devastating part of it all was? When they took me into his office that day, there was a song playing, by a singer called Fairuz. It was a song I really love, called "Yesterday's Encounter." When they took me back to solitary after I'd smoked, I was humming the song. I felt like I'd snatched a moment of humanity out of the hell I was in. But then, suddenly, as I was squatting on the floor to sleep, because there wasn't enough space to lie down, I burst into tears. It was the hardest moment of my whole time in detention. I was thinking how that interrogator must wake up in the morning, have a cup of tea, smoke a cigarette, kick back, listen to Fairuz. He must be a normal person like me. So how could he do that to us? How could they create a place like that? I cried so hard that night I could barely breathe.

(*Silence.*)

ANAS: The bastard stole the song. I haven't been able to listen to it since I got out.

SCENE 7

SETTING: *Two days after the previous meetings, in the same offices.*

THOMAS: I've written down here that you said your first arrest took place in May 2011, at a protest. You spent thirteen days in detention. Your second arrest took place in June 2012.

You spend sixty days at the branch where Walid Salem was an interrogator with the rank of major. Correct?

ANAS: Correct.

THOMAS: In your interview with the Bundesamt für Migration und Flüchtlinge in 2015, you talked about these periods of detention, but you gave different figures for the durations. You said you spent a month in detention on the first occasion, and four months on the second.

ANAS: Really?

. . . .

(*WALID is holding a small monstera plant in a ceramic pot. He hands it to NADIA.*)

MAHA: Baba's brought you a cutting of his monstera plant as a gift. You're getting one of his babies.

NADIA: Thanks so much, it's gorgeous!

WALID: I thought I'd give you this one because it's nice and strong. Wherever you put it, it'll fight to stay alive and keep growing.

. . . .

THOMAS (*holding up a piece of paper*): In this interview from 2016, you say the first time lasted a month and a half, and the second time lasted around six months.

ANAS: I don't remember talking about being arrested with the Bundesamt, or with the journalist. They might have written it down wrong. I really don't know.

. . . .

NADIA (*flicking through her papers*): Yesterday I was going through the statements you made to the German police in 2015. There's actually quite a few things I need to clear up with you. For example, you've said to me more than once that from the end of April 2011 you sensed a clear change in the branch chief's level of trust in you. You felt like you yourself were under surveillance, and as a result, your authority diminished tangibly. But in February 2015, you said that in May 2012, you came to blows with another officer in the branch because you had given orders for a number of detainees to be released. He objected on the grounds the decision was premature, but you insisted, and the detainees were released. Correct?

MAHA: That's what happened, yes.

NADIA: Don't you think there's a contradiction between that, and what you were saying about your authority being undermined? You say your position within the branch essentially became a formality, a token—and yet a year later, you were still able to impose your authority regarding something as significant as the release of several detainees.

(*MAHA looks at WALID as if expecting a response, but he says nothing.*)

NADIA: Okay, let's move on. In the same statement, another thing caught my eye.

MAHA: When you're describing the situation in the branch in 2012, you say, "What were interrogators like us meant to do with dead detainees?" What did you mean by that?

WALID: It's obvious what I meant. I was criticizing the brutal treatment to which detainees were subject.

NADIA: Honestly, when I read it, it sounded to me like you meant you were frustrated that this was standing in the way of your work as an interrogator.

MAHA (*taking over*): As in, you wanted the detainees alive so you could interrogate them. Because that was your job.

WALID: That's her interpretation. But what I said was clear. I was criticizing the fact they killed the detainees.

....

THOMAS: You told me about a method they called "al-shabih." In your interview with the Bundesamt für Migration und Flüchtlinge you mentioned that you were left with pains in your feet and legs for a long time after being subjected to this method of torture. As far as I can see from what I've read about it, it causes damage to the wrists and shoulders, sometimes permanent. But not to the legs.

ANAS: It says that about the feet and legs?

THOMAS (*shows ANAS a piece of paper*): That's what it says here in the BAMF interview, verbatim.

ANAS (*examining the paper*): It was probably a mistake by the interpreter. My German wasn't very good back then, so I had to trust the interpreter. I remember I wasn't very happy with him.

THOMAS: Why didn't you request a different one? You have the right to change interpreters.

ANAS: I just wanted to get it over and done with. Do you

know how long you have to wait to get a BAMF appointment? You know your entire fate as a refugee rests on that interview?

. . . .

NADIA: Okay, but you need to be aware that things you've said in official contexts will be followed up on. Also, just as a reminder, you made this statement voluntarily when you approached the police in February 2015 to report that you suspected you were being followed by the Syrian intelligence services. I must say what most surprised me is that you signed your statement using your former rank: Major Walid Salem.

MAHA: You never told me about that.

WALID: About what? Translate what she said!

MAHA: That you were followed by the Syrian intelligence in Berlin and that you went to the police to report it. Why have you never told me that?

WALID: We can talk about that later.

MAHA: How can you hide something like that from me?

WALID: I just had some suspicions at the time, and I didn't want you and your mother to have to live in fear.

MAHA: Why didn't you tell me about it when you were arrested? It's not like it's a minor detail.

WALID: Maha, my head's already going to explode from all the questions. Don't make it worse.

MAHA: Baba, I need to know things that are going to affect the case. I can't just find out something like this in passing.

NADIA: Shall we take a break?

WALID (*simultaneously*): Yes.

MAHA (*simultaneously*): No.

WALID: Tea?

NADIA: Sure.

MAHA: No.

WALID: Coffee?

MAHA (*raising her voice*): Can we please continue?

(*Silence.*)

MAHA: I'd like to see a copy of the statement you're talking about.

. . . .

THOMAS: So were you really subjected to al-shabih?

. . . .

MAHA: In the same statement, you describe your work at the branch. You say, "I conducted high-intensity interrogations. There were occasions when it wasn't possible to be civil." Could you give me an example?

WALID (*irritated*): What do you mean, an example? How many times do I have to explain? We're going round in circles here. I told you, there was a role I had to play within the branch. I had to keep it up until the moment came when we could get out of the country, so you and your mother would be safe. Was I meant to stand up in front of them all and announce I was defecting? And now I'm here in Germany, and they're telling me how things are meant to work in Syria. What do they know about how the Syrian intelligence services work? And by the way, do you think everyone who came into the branch was a peaceful protestor? There were people who were worse than the regime. They'd have done worse things than the regime if they were given half the chance. Some of them had to be crushed.

MAHA: Crushed?

NADIA: Could you translate what he just said?

MAHA: Just a second. How did you crush them?

WALID: Now you're questioning me too?

NADIA: What's the issue here?

MAHA: Just a second, please. I'd like to know how you crushed the ones who had to be crushed.

WALID: You of all people know I couldn't crush an ant. I'm sick of having this conversation. Listen, there were innocent people who shouldn't have been there. But there were also criminals and terrorists. Over here, they send drones to go and kill them. Do you get it now?

NADIA: I'm sorry, but I need to know what you're talking about. Or I can give you five minutes if you'd like.

WALID: Tell her I want to move on. She needs to get in touch with the people whose numbers I gave her. She can use them as witnesses, because they helped me defect and get to Germany.

. . . .

ANAS (*getting up to leave*): I don't want to continue. The questions you're asking today—it's like you don't believe what I'm saying.

THOMAS: I'm checking the details, that's all.

(*Silence.*)

THOMAS: Look, Anas. Our task here isn't to prove that the regime was barbaric. Walid Salem himself agrees the regime was barbaric. That's why he defected, right? Our task is to prove that Walid Salem participated in that barbarity, even though he's trying to distance himself from it now. To do that, our account has to be supported by factual evidence. If we want to lose, then sure, we can present an account full of mistakes.

ANAS (*sitting down again opposite THOMAS*): What about all the psychological damage Walid Salem left me with? Does that count as factual evidence? Panic attacks, do they count? And how do I prove to the court that the tone of that man's voice was the tone of someone who believed in what they were doing, who enjoyed what they were doing?

. . . .

NADIA: Listen to me, please, both of you. I'm afraid I don't understand everything you're saying. But I'd like to share what I've been thinking about for the last few days. Since we first met, it's been clear to me that you'd like to base your defense on the notion you're completely innocent. Because you didn't torture Anas Jaber or any other detainee at the branch in the period preceding your defection, nor did you give orders for torture to take place. The factual basis for this claim is that your position within the branch had been reduced to a matter of appearance—partly because there were doubts about your loyalty, and partly because detainees were brought to you as a formality, as a routine procedure, whether they were to be held at the branch or transferred somewhere else. Is that more or less correct?

MAHA: Correct.

WALID: What's correct?

MAHA: She's just summarizing what you've said so far. There's nothing new.

NADIA: To be perfectly honest, I'm finding this narrative inconsistent. Essentially, I'm seeing two people here. The first is the one who appears in the statement you made voluntarily to the police in 2015. That person sensed he was being followed in Berlin by the Syrian intelligence services, and the statement he made suggests he enjoyed considerable authority within his branch up until the point he defected. The second person, meanwhile, is telling me now that he was a marginal figure whose position was largely a formality. Regardless of which of these is correct, what we do know is that you were an interrogator in the branch during the period in which Anas Jaber and other former detainees are alleging you played a role in the abuses to which they were subjected.

(*NADIA looks toward MAHA, expecting her to translate, but MAHA says nothing.*)

NADIA: To decide if I can continue to represent you, I need you to help me get to know you better. I need to know who you are. So far, it feels like you're not helping me.

(*NADIA and WALID look toward MAHA, waiting for her to translate. Silence. MAHA leans back in her chair and takes a cigarette from her bag.*)

MAHA: Okay if I smoke?

(*MAHA lights the cigarette without waiting for an answer.*)

WALID: You smoke?

(*MAHA nods, exhaling a cloud of smoke.*)

WALID: Since when?

(*MAHA offers a cigarette to NADIA, who takes it. MAHA lights it for her. WALID looks stunned. NADIA looks uncomfortable. MAHA bursts out laughing.*)

WALID: I didn't expect to find out you'd been smoking behind my back.

(*WALID picks up the monstera plant, removing it from the path of the cigarette smoke, and places it at a distance.*)

MAHA (*still laughing*): We're clearly all still getting to know each other. (*Continues to laugh as she addresses NADIA.*) I've been scared of this moment my whole life. I've imagined hundreds of scenarios. The moment Baba finds out that I smoke… I never thought it would be like this. (*Still laughing.*)

NADIA (*trying not to laugh too*): I was always scared to smoke in front of my dad too. Even though I know that he knows that I know that he knows—

(*NADIA and MAHA both burst out laughing.*)

MAHA: —That I know that he knows that I know that he knows—

(*NADIA and MAHA laugh for a few moments more, then calm down.*)

WALID: Are you finished?

(*MAHA nods, putting out her cigarette.*)

WALID: Can you please translate what she said?

MAHA: I will, afterward.

WALID: Why are you here if you don't want to translate? You need to tell her I'm the victim of a political game. They want to scapegoat me, so they can pretend they're taking steps to hold the regime accountable. You know what that's called? Bullshit. The regime is still sitting there, just how it's always been, in fact even more secure than before. And meanwhile they want to prosecute me because it looks good, when I risked my life, and my family's lives, to defect.

MAHA (*to NADIA*): I'm sorry, I can't translate any more.

(*MAHA stands up and turns to WALID.*)

MAHA: Baba, I need to go outside for a walk. I'll see you at home.

SCENE 14

SETTING: *The kitchen in NADIA's flat. She has invited BASEL to come over. They haven't seen each other since their last argument. We hear*

*the Fairuz song "I Gathered Up the Memory of Yesterday's Encounter"
playing, then NADIA opens the door to let BASEL in and they walk
through to the kitchen. The small monstera plant is on the table.*

BASEL (*looking at the plant*): A new plant? And listening to
Fairuz? This is new.

NADIA (*returning to the cooking*): Baba's been on my mind all
day. He loved Fairuz. This is his favorite out of all her songs.
Do you like Fairuz?

BASEL: Pffff... We have a complicated relationship.

NADIA: The food's nearly ready.

BASEL: Can I help with anything?

NADIA: You can make some salad if you really want.

BASEL: It's my destiny to cook here even when I'm a guest.

(*BASEL stands so close to NADIA that they're touching, then starts
to chop the vegetables.*)

NADIA: I'm glad you came.

BASEL: How are you?

NADIA: Feeling a bit of a mess these days. Tired.

BASEL: Because of work?

(*NADIA says nothing, and they continue to prepare the meal.*)

BASEL: You should be careful you don't get burnout. I've decided to reduce my hours from next month, I was thinking—

NADIA (*interrupting*): Baba left Syria in 1980 because his life was in danger.

(*Silence.*)

NADIA: People in his neighborhood were saying he was responsible for the intelligence services arresting some of their neighbors. Two brothers who were Muslim Brotherhood sympathizers. Apparently they'd been harassing Baba because he was with the regime. They disappeared, and a rumor went round saying it was because Baba had reported them. That was when he decided to leave Syria. He came to Germany, then at some point he met Mom and they got married.

(*Silence.*)

NADIA: And just like you, he never looked back.

BASEL: Who told you that?

NADIA: One of the prosecution lawyers in the Walid Salem case. We've known each other for ages.

(*Silence.*)

NADIA: I called Mom and asked if she knew the story. She said it was a lie they'd made up about Baba, but people believed it. He was still devastated about it when he died, but he never mentioned it. When she told me that I began to understand better why he never visited Syria after leaving, and why he kept me away from everything that was connected to Syria.

BASEL: I'm sorry. I told you this case was going to bring up lots of headaches.

NADIA: Imagine, I've gone through my whole life without knowing about the events that changed his life and led to me being born.

BASEL: Let's go away somewhere. Take a break from work, from Berlin.

NADIA: I don't want to run away.

BASEL: Are you still doing the Walid Salem case?

NADIA: It feels like his story has a lot in common with my father's. What if Walid was made to pay the price for a crime he didn't commit? Even when he fled his country?

BASEL: Please quit this case. Don't get caught up in comparisons like that.

NADIA: Basel, please, can we not go back to the same subject all over again? I don't get why this case bothers you so much.

BASEL: Because I was detained at the same branch where Major Walid Salem was an interrogator. I was there. I saw death. And I saw things worse than death.

NADIA: What? You were arrested?

BASEL: Yes. And I don't think I've ever got out.

NADIA: How come you've never told me this?

BASEL: Because I wanted to forget about the whole nightmare. But it's pointless. It's like a curse. I'm never going to get away from it.

NADIA: Who even am I to you if you can't tell me something like that?

BASEL: What should I have told you? That I was arrested by chance? I'm not a hero or an activist. Everybody around me was braver than me. All I did was help them with some digital security issues. And if I'd thought for a moment it was going to get me arrested, I wouldn't have done it. I'm a coward. I was arrested by chance, and I got out with a bribe. Is that what I was meant to tell you?

NADIA: What, did you think I was going to judge you if you told me?

(*The saucepan of pasta on the stove starts to boil over.*)

BASEL: You want me to tell you? (*Takes the saucepan off the heat and places it next to NADIA.*) Okay, this is what the cell was like. It was smaller than this kitchen, and there were dozens of us stuffed in there, half-naked and with open, festering wounds. If you stood up, you'd lose your spot and you wouldn't be able to sit down again. There was a four-teen-year-old boy in there with us, and I can still hear the sound of his screams. They stuck a gun barrel up my ass; the guard was standing behind me, playing with my chest hair. Why would I want to talk about all that? Why can't I just forget?

NADIA: And Walid Salem was in that branch when you were arrested. Did he interrogate you? Was he responsible for you being tortured?

BASEL: I only found out his name after I got out.

NADIA: How?

BASEL: My dad told me Walid Salem was involved in getting me released. He was grateful to him.

NADIA: So he helped?

BASEL: You have to get over this obsession with Walid Salem.

NADIA: I need to know. Did he help you? Torture you? Blackmail your family? What role did he play exactly?

BASEL: All I know is what I just told you. What my father said about him was positive, but he didn't elaborate, and I didn't want to find out more. For the past ten years, I've been doing everything I can to forget that I was ever inside that place. And all you're doing is taking me back there.

NADIA: I'm so sorry. I'm sorry for everything. I'm sorry I couldn't earn your trust enough for you to share all this pain with me.

BASEL: Don't be sorry. That's exactly why I never talk about getting arrested. I don't want pity. I don't want to be a victim. Victims remain imprisoned, even when they're out. And please, from this moment on, I don't want to hear anything else about this case. I don't want to force you to choose between your job and our relationship, but I can't lie to myself and to you. I can't continue this relationship as long as this case is part of our lives.

(*Silence.*)

Thanks for the invitation. I have to go now.

(*BASEL leaves.*)

SCENE 16

SETTING: *The end of a panel event about the WALID SALEM trial.*

(*ANAS is talking to a female JOURNALIST while BASEL waits at a distance.*)

ANAS: Of course, the fight to document and record is a crucial part of the fight for justice. That's why I started thinking about putting together a book that would record the events of the trial, and all the backstory, from the moment I was detained in Syria to the moment I met Major Walid Salem by chance in Berlin.

JOURNALIST: Well, I can tell you already that I'm really looking forward to reading it. Thanks for your time.

ANAS: Thanks for your interest.

(*The JOURNALIST leaves and ANAS turns to BASEL, who has been waiting for him to finish.*)

BASEL: Your talk was really interesting. Thanks for doing it.

ANAS: Thanks for coming.

BASEL: I'm Basel. From Syria. I think we have some common friends.

ANAS: Why are we speaking German then?

BASEL: I find it more comfortable, if you don't mind. When I came to Germany, I had to learn German really quickly for work. Now it feels like I can express myself better in German than in Arabic.

ANAS: They don't take you seriously in this country until you speak the language. Everything changes when you show them you can stand up for yourself in German. So who are our common friends?

BASEL: Do you know Nadia Majed? The lawyer?

ANAS: Not personally, no.

BASEL: Okay, well, I'd like you not to talk so much about her and her family. Her father died a long time ago, and he can't defend himself. And as a person who's fighting for justice, I know you'd agree that's not right.

ANAS: I'm sorry, what?

BASEL: You heard me. There's no need to go spreading rumors about her private life and her family, and their past. Honestly, it's below the belt. I mean, I'm sure you wouldn't want people talking about your history of sexual harassment and assault against women, right?

ANAS: You're accusing me of assault?

BASEL: Me? Of course not. I'm just reminding you what people used to say about you in Lebanon. And Turkey. Right? The people who said that are still around. Oh, and now you mention common friends—remember Adam Saleh? He told me that you being detained was all a coincidence. You weren't an activist or anything. It was the first time you'd even gone to that office, which was being watched because a bunch of naive activists used to meet there. He also told me about the hard drive. Remember? Videos of demonstrations that people had risked their lives to record. He trusted you so he gave it to you to pass on to someone. But you didn't pass it on, you kept it, and you used a bunch of the footage and pretended it was your work. Adam's still around, we can ask him.

ANAS: You and whoever's behind you are liars. Whoever's sent you here is obviously trying to undermine the credibility of the witnesses and the trial. But you are not going to stand in the way of justice.

BASEL: Spare me the crap about justice—it doesn't do it for me. But I wish you every success. Don't go thinking I'm worried about Walid Salem. I wish they'd execute him. I've just come here to tell you very respectfully to keep Nadia Majed and her family out of it, because she's got nothing to do with all this. Okay?

ANAS: I'm not going to waste any more time with you.

(*ANAS leaves.*)

BASEL (*out loud*): Ciao. Let's hope we don't have to meet again.

SAY GOODBYE
TO NINA

by RABAB HAIDAR

THE DRIZZLING MADE THE old basalt stones that paved the dark alley shiny, slithery, and almost impossible to trust. In the corner was the small statue of a white ceramic Virgin Mary in a blue robe. Her body was encircled in ceramic roses. A dead serpent under her left foot, and her arms outstretched spreading blessings to the passersby. Next to her was a flickering candle that cast amber light over the shrine. It was a globe of amber light.

Behind this shrine, in a pitch-black void, the light of more shrines floated in midair.

A man approached me with a big smile. I felt light. I felt happy. I followed the bubbles of words coming out of his mouth as they burst. The man came closer. He smiled as I was pushed out of the dream.

I recognized the man from a previous dream. He knew me, but I did not know him. In front of the shrine, in the dark alley, there were many people from the dream world. They were walking, talking to each other, and smiling. I used to live in this alley. It's one of the many alleys forming the gridiron paths of the ancient Christian quarter in Damascus. Despite the many cities I've lived in, although it is not where I was born, Damascus is the city I dwell in in my dreams.

It is the fifth of October, five minutes before the alarm goes off at seven a.m. From my bed, I can see the sky of Berlin dark and leaden, the raindrops cascading down the windowpane. It has been raining for days, and it is damp and cold. The weather report predicts heavy snow for the upcoming week. My mobile screen flashes: a message on my phone from a woman I do not know well. We have sat and talked a couple of times before, on occasions where you must sit and talk to people "Your brain, ah, your brain" the woman had interrupted me from the other side of the table the first time we met, clenching her teeth and curling her fingers, with her arms stretched toward me. The next time we met she declared that we were friends, and I chose not to argue with that.

"Heyyyyy, my dear, good mooorning," the text message reads. "First of all, unfortunately, I cannot see you as much as I would like to!! I am with colleagues—academics! from the university where I've been invited to lecture. My love, concerning our project to get funding, you just have to write what you said to me the other day, with the keyword 'cross-cultural.' The deadline is a few days, but we can do it. Don't forget: cross-cultural. I miss you so much, kisses and hugs."

"Cross-cultural" is the new keyword for obtaining a grant. Before "cross-cultural," the keywords were "refugees" and "integration." Then the words became "feminism" and "empowering women."

I have half an hour to leave the house for the German course.

The internet does not give a clear answer to why people have recurring dreams. But on a website promoting wellness, in a video with gentle trickling water and wafting flute sounds in the background, a life coach recommends a breathing meditation before sleep. A famous internet doctor with a well-pressed, clean green surgical robe recommends two drops of edible lavender oil in a morning cup of water and one spoon of coconut oil in a cup of coffee. An online gynecologist agrees with the coconut oil and promises this trick will solve the hormonal problem most probably responsible for inadequate sleep.

I throw the raincoat over my oversized winter jacket and leave the house. On my way to the nearby underground train station, I check in my waterproof bag for my mobile phone, keys, and notebook. The class is starting in less than thirty minutes.

The station is quiet despite the many people waiting for the underground train. The yellow U-Bahn arrives packed with employees heading to their offices carrying long faces, heavy backpacks, coffee mugs, and croissants in brown paper bags. When they get to their offices there will be piles and piles of papers and checks. They will repeat the weather report to each other, sign more papers, stamp and send. I assume.

Oversized winter jackets crowd the stained gray and blue inner cabin of the U-Bahn. For one reason or another, we keep a decent distance from each other. We stare at each other and at those who stare at their mobiles, keeping smiles carefully locked in place.

We used to smile to each other back in Syria— did we smile, in the streets, in offices, and on public transport? Or am I remembering a non-existent past?

In my third year of college, my father gave me a small sum of money to buy a car. I wanted a classic, curvy, cozy used Volkswagen Beetle with a large steering wheel. I dreamed of painting it green. My friend Tony argued that old cars need constant maintenance, that they are expensive and impractical, and my father agreed. Thus, I got my first made-in-Korea car, shiny silver with a small electrical sunroof, a small overhead compartment for sunglasses, front lights the shape of the eyes of a cat, and three years of monthly payments for the bank.

Tony was a property manager permitted by the local authorities to work within the Christian quarter of old Damascus. He helped tourists and students find apartments and saw to it that vacant apartments were rented. If you were a new student in Damascus, within two to three days, Tony could find you a room to rent or at least a closet. Sometimes, those closets or rooms were under unstable historical staircases. The stability of the staircase above one's room depended on how much one's parents were able to pay.

The owners of the homes usually kept the first floor of the houses, with their inner courtyards and their fountains, to themselves and rented the rest of the rooms out.

Sometimes, the house was too good to abandon and too worn to renovate, prompting the owners' decision to depart to the nearby, relatively new, somehow elegant quarter of Qassaa, leaving Tony in charge. Some old historical houses turned into family restaurants, cozy bars, and small nightclubs that filled the narrow streets with colorful lights, visitors, tourists, strollers, cars, layered sounds of music, laughter, and sounds of forks and knives dinging porcelain dishes and clunking glasses, shisha smoke mixed with scents of food and women's and men's perfumes.

Tony was trusted by the homeowners, the students' parents, the police, and the Secret Service. He kept the latter informed of the activities of the tourists and the local residents, and he would sometimes tell us, and the neighbors, all about it. Sometimes, he helped the police corner a thief, and afterward he would strut in between the houses, throwing his thin, long legs in front of him, tall and proud. He collected rent on time, maintained safety, discipline, and good spirit among us, his subjects, and kept the candles lit in the Virgin Mary shrines around the corner from the houses he managed.

Tony was a loyal subject to the Monastery of Our Lady of Saidnaya, where he was born in a two-story house nestled among the hills that the monastery overlooked. His mother and four sisters still lived in the same house, and he visited them regularly. Tony loved his mother, two of his sisters, his country, his cigarettes, and driving six-wheelers.

Tony was a great driver, according to his own stories. One time, he drove a six-wheel truck backward from the hills of Saidnaya to Abbasyeen Square. Tony told us this in a deep and dry voice while holding an imaginary steering wheel and looking behind his bony wide shoulders into an imaginary road. This was likely impossible, we thought, as that would be seventeen kilometers of driving backward, on a sloping, winding road, but we did not tell Tony most of what we thought.

Tony's real passion was carving small wooden figurines of women in traditional Damascene dresses. The figurines had handmade metal crosses hanging from their necks that dropped between two voluptuous, nippled breasts. Their faces were round, and they had big hazel-coloured eyes. He sold his wooden ladies to tourists and foreigners living in Bab Tuma— studying Arabic, Sufism, religion, the local economy—and to us. Although Tony sold his figurines to foreigners and helped them find rooms to rent, he did not trust them. He was highly suspicious of their motives. He pressured us not to mingle with them and pressured the Secret Service to investigate them. He provided evidence to the Secret Service to back up his suspicions, so much so that the Secret Service eventually told him to calm down.

We, the local students, loved the tourists and foreign students; we loved talking to them and befriending them, cooking for them and seeing the *wow* in their eyes. We liked their genuine surprise at our way of life. We tried to keep surprising them and observed them as they observed us. The Germans dressed like hippies. Although relaxed and friendly, they kept a careful distance and had a low profile. The Americans were not cautious at all; they made a splash wherever they went, and we loved them for that. The Spanish were louder and more chaotic than us, lived in big groups, and mixed with each other. The British came and left and moved individually. They had keen eyes for details and kept clear of the Americans. Some Italians acted like Americans, some Austrians acted like the British, and some Germans acted like us. After some time, we could roughly figure out who an ordinary international student was and who was in Damascus aiming to join the diplomatic corps back home. But we kept those observations to ourselves. We did not want Tony to be more suspicious than he already was.

One or two of Tony's dolls ended up in small European exhibitions; some local journalists wrote a couple of impressions. Tony, who had never aimed for Europe, liked the photos of his work in foreign magazines and asked me to translate what was written under the pictures. Pleased, he listened while smoking his local tobacco and drinking dark black tea.

Tony believed I was better than any foreign young man who dared to show interest in me or whom I showed interest in.

"Do you know how many college degrees she has?" he would tell the interested man or the neighbors, pointing at me with his two fingers holding a crooked cigarette. "Do you know how many languages she speaks?"

At the time, I had only two college bachelor's degrees, had no master's degree and zero PhDs, and spoke only two languages, but Tony was very proud of me. My father was also proud of me, and some of my friends who spoke one language were proud or even jealous, even if they had fairer skin, which was a big advantage that I missed, according to my mother. My mother was proud too, but only sometimes.

Was Tony the man in my dream? I don't think so. Yet, looking back on my dream, I am sure I saw one of Tony's dolls walking around in the background.

I am already late for my German course and still have one more station on the U-Bahn and four minutes to walk to reach the class.

Twenty minutes late, I storm into class. The teacher is not there. My fellow students are silent; the air is charged. Hussein, who is twenty-eight and from Afghanistan and the youngest refugee student in our class, stands angrily; his face is tomato red. He looks at me as he throws his arms in the air and complains, "Nicht nett, Nein, Nicht nett!"

"What is it?" I ask, shaking my head as a sign language. I do not share a language with Hussein. I do not share a language with Ali either. Ali is Hussein's friend. He's sixty years old, the oldest in the class, and he shakes his head in solidarity with Hussein.

I share fewer things than a language with the women of the class, who are diplomatically silent. I share even fewer things with the men who choose to shut their eyes to any incident that might jeopardize their aspirations to survive this four-month course, no matter how bad the situation is: to endure and survive, to achieve the long life of prosperity promised to them and their families on this land.

The teacher who is preparing us to integrate into our new life in Germany told us, "You are here to be the workers that this country is missing. Old people are old, and young people like to sit at their computers and create companies and great plans."

It was not a nasty statement compared to what I jokingly started to call "the statement of the day" from the beginning of the course twenty-one days ago.

The first sentences our teacher spoke that made me shiver were "I am Catholic. I put my kids in Catholic kindergarten. I would maybe put them in Protestant school. But I would never, never put them with Muslims. I am not racist, but I do not like terrorists, who bomb and kill..." The women diplomatically kept silent, and the men closed their eyes. I objected to the racist stereotype, and Nina, another student in the course, from her desk behind me, with a louder voice and distinctive Russian accent, asked the teacher to show more respect in the class.

In another statement the following day, the teacher, who was taking care of our integration into the Market, said, "We Christians write from left to right. Muslims write from right to left."

"What about the writing from top to bottom?" I sarcastically said in English. The teacher ignored me, and Nina laughed, flipping her hair back.

"Wait! Where is Nina?"

Nina escaped Siberia for Russia and then escaped Russia for Israel, where she had a child. Then she, with her little son, escaped Israel for Germany. These are her words, not mine. Nina wears high heels and colorful skirts.

I had to lose my high heels to maintain the speed of scurrying and bustling, following the routes of underground Berlin lines and buses on Google Maps. I scurry from the federal office of employment to the lawyer. I fill out endless forms to prove that I am integrating. The system is working well for me! Piles and piles of paper, despite the protests every summer where young activists glue their hands to the hot asphalt of the main streets of Berlin protesting the slaughtering of trees—piles of piles of papers I have to fill!

Nina storms into the class and flips her long gray and blond hair away from her face. Nina wears the most elegant earrings. They are well designed, balanced, polished, in shades of off-gold or golden-rose. Today's earrings are big flat round golden flowers, flickering light on her face. Nina says, "Ah, you are here! We are all here! We should not have to deal with this tardiness from this man."

"Of course," I say, as the teacher, the thick bold blond man, storms in behind Nina, squinting his blue eyes behind his glasses. He shouts, "No riots in my class! Sit down, sit down!"

Nina stands taller than him in her high heels. Hussein stands by his desk to my right, and in solidarity, Ali stands beside him. I am standing among them all, still holding my metal cup of coffee; the grease of the coconut oil is evident on the cup's lip.

"I don't know why you are so hostile toward me," says the teacher to Nina, ignoring Ali, Husein, and me.

"I myself am an immigrant; I came to Berlin from Hungary in the late eighties."

Of course he is! I should have guessed this; I have already observed the prejudice that immigrants of different backgrounds have for one another. It's a harsh and acute prejudice that casts the false question of who has the right to survive!

The teacher looks at Nina and addresses her in Russian in an attempt to find mutual ground with her. He keeps ignoring Ali, Hussein, and me, but Nina shouts to him as she points at me, "Talk to me in English, in front of a witness." I am Nina's witness.

The teacher storms out. Nina shakes her beautiful golden flower earrings.

"Now we go to the administration and request a new teacher," says Nina. "He has been disrespectful. He is misogynistic toward women and hateful against you guys."

I do not ask her to identify "you guys." We are Muslim and Christians and Zoroastrians, Egyptian, Iranian, Afghan, Syrian, and Lebanese, and one Jamaican, shades from dark brown all the way to pale champagne!

I say instead, "Of course, the administration has to know."

"Let's go," says Nina.

Hussein and Ali are ready to march. The men in the class awaken, survey the scene, and declare, "If you go, we go." A polite woman echoes, "If you go, I go."

"Wait!" I interject. "You and I speak English, but the Arabs do not speak English or Persian, the Persians and Afghans do not speak Arabic or English, and no one speaks German. Note that the administration refuses to use a language other than German! If we go now, we will jam the small office of the administrator like a small, unintelligible carnival babbling different languages while throwing our arms in the air. We won't be able to communicate. We should write an email, and thus we register our complaints."

"No, we're going now!" Nina says and frowns so the lines of crow's feet around her eyes grow deeper.

"No, an email." I say, then I reiterate the importance of communication and the legality of email. Nina, frustrated by my too-much-logic, storms out. I storm out after her. Ali and Hussein are following me; following us are the future workers of this country, anxious not to miss any crucial updates.

We stand outside. I light a cigarette, as do some of the carnival members. Nina leaves us frustrated. I shortly leave the mute group, going back home. The U-Bahn is not that full, my metal cup of coffee with coconut oil is still half full, the idea of sending an email sounds legit, yet it is not!

I keep believing that writing an email is the right choice for a couple of more hours until I am in bed that night. I randomly watch videos on my phone: clips from *The Office*, *Bob's Burgers*, *Seinfeld*, something to make me laugh. It occurs to me that the email might not be a bridge but an obstacle.

The future workers do not have emails, they mostly use Facebook Messenger. To many, the email sounds unsavory and passive-aggressive. When one has objections, one gathers their friends and confronts the other, eye to eye. Thus, an email is a stab in the back. It is, I guess, connected to the idea of reports written by friends and family to the Secret Service, a tradition still kept alive by many governments from not too long ago, from the era of Cold War.

Besides, a school for Ausländers, future workers that this land needs, that does not have one person to speak a common language with its students deserves a visit from our small carnival, us shaking our heads, pointing fingers, speaking five different languages they have to find a way to understand.

Tomorrow, I will accompany Nina and Hussein to the administration office.

"Breathe!"

Did the man in my dream ask me to breathe? The man who knows me, whom I met in a previous dream.

A few minutes before the alarm clock goes off, I open my eyes and watch yet another dream slip away. Something important was said in this dream that I cannot carry with me into my waking day. Another missed message!

The alarm clock goes off. The mobile screen flashes, displaying the time and date. It is seven o'clock in the morning on October 6, 2023.

I have a text message from the friend who likes my brain: "Gooood morning beautiful. The lecture I am giving starts early today, so I thought I would wake you up. ;) Did you think of something for us? The deadline is in a few days! Just write what you said about colliding among cultures, collision, collective ego... and your theory of... immigrants? You know! What you said the other day. We need a simple outline titled 'Cross-Culture' something, with a couple of keywords on the subject... You know how to do it!"

The sky is dark, covered in one big heavy leaden cloud, with raindrops cascading down the window next to my bed. I have half an hour to leave the house. One tablespoon of coconut oil goes in my coffee, a few drops of lavender oil in my morning cup of water, and the raincoat goes over my winter jacket. The air is damp and misty, and the underground station is quiet and gray.

Nina does not attend the class today, the future workers are sitting in fraught silence with their eyes closed: to endure and survive, to achieve the long life of prosperity promised to them and their families on this land. The short thick man squinting his blue eyes from behind his glasses ignores my presence. "No riots in my class" still echoing on the wall.

Having to explain to the job center why I declined taking a class under such conditions would be more traumatic than facing one thick short man, even without Nina by my side. Nina did not attend today's class. Next week Nina, Hussein, and I will go to the administration.

October 7, the dream wakes me up at three a.m. and then fades away quickly. I go back to bed at eight. It is Saturday, which means time can disappear and reappear throughout the day as it pleases. In between I watch passages of *The Office*, *Seinfeld*, and video reels. A man with the Palestinian flag veiling his face to dance, toe-heel jump, and stamp, fire in the background. Palestine is rising again. I watch the video on repeat. The man is in every video on my "for you" page.

It is Sunday, the eighth of October. I follow the news and the dancing man. The world is freaking out.

Who has the right to survive?

"Anti-Semitism" is the new keyword.

Monday, the ninth of October, the dream that keeps slipping away from me wakes me up at five a.m. I check the news on Palestine. I leave comments of worry on videos, pictures, and the online message boards, despite warnings from friends and the government not to interact; Ausländers have to show their goodwill to integrate with the core-wound of the new Land.

I put one big spoon of coconut oil in my coffee and a few drops of lavender oil in my water. I receive a text message from the friend who likes to eat my brain, "Hello dear, I am starting to worry about you. Are you fine? Have you found a title for our project yet? The deadline for funding the project is in two days!! Just record what you said the other day about immigrants and collisions between cultures. Write what you said the other day! A simple outline—once we are granted the funds, you and I can work from there! I love you so much. Hugs and kisses."

In the background of my dream, there was the dancing man. Viva Palestina's song was playing. What was I doing? Whom did I see? There was a different smiling man. He gave me a book with codes. I needed to keep the book with me at all times to decode something. What is the thing I need to decipher?

One aspirin for the headache, one coconut oil for my coffee, and a few drops of edible lavender oil in my morning cup of water. The weather is cold and damp. The underground metro is jammed. Nina is again absent. The German teacher looks thicker and denser. He moves more nervously than before. He squints his eyes. The dancing man in the video from Palestine is still trending.

In the break, one silent woman stands next to me. Carefully, she murmurs, "Rumor has it, Nina asked to be transferred from our class because she feared for herself as an Israeli among us!"

"I don't believe it," I say. "Nina disagreed with the Israeli government. She escaped Israel—those were her words."

The woman answers carefully, "Maybe. But it is easier to say you are scared of Arabs and Muslims than to accuse a German teacher of racism!"

"Are you sure of this?" I ask.

"It's impossible to tell for sure," the woman answers and slides back to the class.

I stay outside and smoke a second cigarette alone. Class starts. I am five minutes late returning to class after the break. Upon my entrance, the teacher bellows, "There is one God in the sky, and I am your God here in the class!"

"This is ridiculous," I say. I try to laugh, and my objection fades away, like my dreams at night, where there is a book to help me decode something!

At home, in bed, I randomly watch videos on my phone: clips from *The Office*, *Bob's Burgers*, *Seinfeld*, the Palestinian war covered by citizen-journalists, and videos of the dancing man.

Tony lost his real estate business at the beginning of the Syrian War as the foreigners and local students disappeared. However, for his contributions and loyalty, the government gave him a gun and a protective vest so he could become a member of the civil defense army in the alley where we used to live. Tony caught many suspects, all of whom later appeared to be Secret Service members who had undisclosed missions in the Christian quarter, so many that the local authority was left with no choice but to take back his weapon and vest and relieve him from his duties. The government sent him a thank you letter signed by the local chief of Bab Tuma, whom Tony had always disliked; the letter recommended Tony rest at his mother's house next to the Monastery of Lady of Saidnaya, where the air is fresh.

The screen of my cell phone flashes. There is a message from the friend who wants to eat my brain that screams, "ARE YOU TRYING TO SABOTAGE ME? THE DEADLINE IS TOMORROW. YOU KNOW THIS. AND YOU STILL DON'T EVEN HAVE A TITLE!!! ARE YOU JUST LAZY? YOU REFUSE TO ACKNOWLEDGE ME! YOU ARE NOTHING! ABSOLUTELY NOTHING!"

Another message follows, "I will not let you SURRENDER to your depression, dear! I AM HERE TO MOTIVATE YOU. I believe in you. You are a brilliant brain. I want you to get up and fight! I love you so much!! The outline is one page. And you had such a fantastic idea that I cannot remember now. Just write it. I believe in you. Do you want to meet tonight? I am having a drink with a friend of mine, a director, a lovely man, but he is married. :(Do you want to join us? We can think together. Do you remember the idea you said before? Can you repeat it? You can talk, and I can just record you. I love you so much."

How did I never get Nina's cell phone number or email? I am sure she did not use "us," whoever "us" is, to justify her need to transfer schools. I am almost sure.

It's another rainy night in Berlin. The rain is delightfully and playfully tapping against my window. The sound of rain slips into my dream. The drizzling makes the basaltic stones that paved old Damascus's alley shiny and slithery. The Virgin

Mary steps on amber spheres of light and kills the evil serpent with her left foot. Her foot floats in a dark void. Beneath the floating spheres, many people are chatting and laughing. Some are waving in my direction. The man who knows me smiles as he approaches me. He is holding a book of codes that I need to decipher.

SLEEPING SONG

by ZAKARIA TAMER
translated by KATHARINE HALLS

WHEN NARIMAN TOLD HER young child, who was clinging to her, to stop talking and go to bed, he begged her to sing to him to help him fall asleep quickly, and since she couldn't remember any of the lullabies she used to know, she instead sang him a song about the king and the king's sons and the king's castles and the king's battles and the king's gold and the king's cars and private jets and yachts, and paintings and statues and songbirds in cages, and the child fell asleep, and in his dreams he saw a black sky and rabid dogs ravaging the face of the water.

Nariman remembered her husband, who had disappeared without trace after divorcing her for no reason, and her depression felt like murky water she couldn't fight off, forcing her under when instead she longed to sing for joy, and though she dismissed this strange longing she found herself compelled, compelled to sing, never mind that there was no one to listen but her black cat, and when the cat heard her singing it stopped its capering and meowing and fell asleep on the spot; astonished at the effect her voice had had, and wanting to be sure, Nariman sang to her mother, who could never sleep without swallowing a handful of sleeping pills, yet she immediately dozed off.

Nariman sang to her father, and her father fell into a deep slumber, snoring lustily, though usually he spent his nights roaming the house like a ghost, his aches and sorrows refusing to let him close his eyes.

Nariman sang to the trees in her gardens; they yawned and stretched, shrugging off their roots, lay down on the ground and abandoned themselves to sleep.

Nariman sang to brooks and streams; their waters ceased flowing, and they gladly drifted off to sleep as if listening to the stories of so many mothers.

Nariman sang to her neighbors, who all went to sleep, along with jailers and jailed, and givers of bribes and takers of bribes, and Nariman grew confident in her singing and its mysterious powers and effects.

Nariman sang to sniggering sons digging graves for still-living parents; sleep assailed them and tossed them into the pits their own hands had dug.

Nariman sang to racehorses as they raced, and they slowed to a trot, but the whips that swatted at their backs forced them to forget their lethargy.

Nariman sang to books, and their words slumbered on white beds.

Nariman sang to chatterers and prattlers, who fell asleep along with their tongues and saw in their dreams that they talked without stopping.

Nariman sang to the comfortable chairs that squatted in the front rows, and the chairs slid out from under their occupants and drifted off to sleep, and the people ululated in joy and put on white clothes.

Nariman sang to fishermen, and the fishermen fell asleep, and birds perched on the mouths of their guns to take snapshots as souvenirs.

Nariman sang to fearful men and the fear went to sleep for a few minutes, then woke again, powerful and eager to lay its hands on more slaves.

Nariman sang to houses with lights in their windows, and when husbands fell asleep their wives discovered that the sky was studded with stars.

Nariman sang to wives killing their husbands in secret, and the wives went to sleep, elated and merry.

Nariman sang to soldiers consumed by killing and genocide and destruction, their guns strafing the skies with missiles determined to spread defeat, and the soldiers staggered, then toppled fast asleep to the blood-spattered, ash-strewn ground, and death, too, fell asleep, and so did the dust and smoke and fire.

Nariman sang to elegantly dressed men who were flaying the skin from the planet and its people and plants and creatures in order to drill for more wealth; the elegantly dressed men went to sleep, and the crude oil gushed forth with no one to possess it and sell it to the highest bidder.

A little girl came running to Nariman, her forlorn wail beseeching her to sing to the unknown men who had kidnapped her father, her one and only, and were planning to kill him, so Nariman hurried to sing to the kidnappers, and not one fell asleep, for they were all deaf, and instead they brayed and bellowed their slogans as they slaughtered their hostage like a starving person slaughters a chicken, and Nariman was saddened and dispirited and grew bitter at her songs and her voice, and forswore her singing; but soon she found herself longing to sing joyfully again, with an unruly longing she was barely able to contain, so she sang to herself, and fell into a long sleep never to be broken by waking.

RASHA ABBAS is a Syrian writer. Born in Latakia and brought up in Damascus, she is currently based in Berlin. She published her first short story collection, *Adam Hates TV*, in 2008. She is also the author of two other short story collections: *The Invention of German Grammar* (2016) and *The Gist of It* (2017). A stage production based on *The Gist of It* was presented at Maxim Gorki Theater in Berlin (2022–2023).

FADWA AL-ABBOUD is a Syrian writer and critic who works in cultural journalism. She has a master's in philosophy and literature. She writes short stories, and her works include *A Hill Inhabited by Enemies* (2022) and *Katara's List: The Hero's Transformations in the Arabic Novel* (2023). She won the Ettijahat Horizons for Deepening Culture Grant for her book *Representations of Identity in the War Novel: A Reading of the Lebanese and Syrian Novel* (2023).

GHADA ALATRASH, PhD, is an assistant professor at the School of Critical and Creative Studies at Alberta University of the Arts in Calgary, Canada. Her current research speaks to Syrian art and creative expression as resistance to oppression and dictatorship.

MUSTAFA TAJ ALDEEN ALMOSA was born in Idlib, Syria, to a working-class family in June 1981. He is the author of six short story collections and four plays. Several of his short stories have been translated into many European languages as well as Turkish, Japanese, Persian, and Kurdish.

KHALIL ALREZ is a Syrian novelist and translator, born in 1956. He has published one play and ten novels, including *A White Cloud in Grandmother's Window* (1998), *Irish Salmon* (2004), *Where Is Safed, Youssef?* (2008), *In Equal Measure* (2014), and most recently *Strawberry-Spotted Handkerchief* (2023). His 2019 novel, *The Russian Quarter*, written in transit from Damascus through Turkey and Greece and finished in Belgium, was shortlisted for the 2020 International Prize for Arabic Fiction; an Italian translation is forthcoming from Einaudi Stile Libero. Alrez's translations from Russian include Evgeny Schwartz's *Tales About Lost Time* (2004), *Selected Russian Short Stories* (2005), and *Selected Stories of Anton Chekhov* (two volumes, 2007). He lives in Brussels.

MOHAMMAD AL ATTAR is a Syrian playwright and essayist. His work takes place on the boundary between fiction and documentation. His plays *Withdrawal*, *Could You Please Look into the Camera?*, *Antigone of Shatila*, *While I Was Waiting*, *Aleppo*, *A Portrait of Absence*, *Iphigenia*, *The Factory*, and *Damascus 2045* were translated into many languages and staged at various locations around the world. He is considered an important chronicler of war-torn Syria.

FADI AZZAM is a Syrian novelist and writer. He is the author of the highly acclaimed novel *Sarmada*, longlisted for the 2012 International Prize for Arabic Fiction. *Huddud's House*, his second novel, was longlisted for the 2018 International Prize for

Arabic Fiction and was translated into English. He was the culture and arts correspondent for *Al-Quds Al-Arabi* newspaper, and his opinion columns have appeared in the *New York Times* and in newspapers across the Middle East.

MARILYN BOOTH is professor emerita, University of Oxford. Her research publications focus on arabophone women's writing and nineteenth-century gender debates, most recently *The Career and Communities of Zaynab Fawwaz: Feminist Thinking in Fin-de-siècle Egypt*. She has translated over twenty works of Arabic fiction, among them *Celestial Bodies* by Omani author Jokha Alharthi, which won the 2019 Man Booker International Prize. Among her other translations are *Bitter Orange Tree* and *Silken Gazelles* by Alharthi; and works by Hoda Barakat, Hassan Daoud, Elias Khoury, Nawal al-Saadawi, and Latifa al-Zayyat.

JAN DOST, born March 12, 1965, in Kobanî, Syria, is a Syrian Kurdish poet, writer, and translator. He has written several novels, both in his native Kurmanji Kurdish language and in Arabic. Several of his novels are set in the context of the Syrian civil war. Apart from his own works, Dost has translated Kurdish and Persian works into Arabic, including *Mem and Zin*, a classical Kurdish love story. His literary contributions span various genres, including poetry, novels, and translations. Some of his works have been translated into Italian, Turkish, Persian, and Spanish. Since 2000, Dost has lived in exile in Germany. He acquired German citizenship in 2008.

SASHA FLETCHER is the author of, most recently, the novel *Be Here to Love Me at the End of the World*. He lives in Brooklyn and can be found online at sashafletcher.info.

RABAB HAIDAR is an author from Syria with a bachelor's degree in English literature. She is a translator, certified by the Ministry of Justice in Damascus, and has translated two books. Her first novel, *Land of Pomegranates*, was published in 2012 amid the Syrian revolution as it transformed into a war. As "a human act of surviving and remembering," Rabab began publishing texts, tales, and articles that reflect on human behavior during times of uncertainty, loss, and fear. Her writings have been translated into German and English. She has participated in numerous literature festivals in Germany and Canada. While in Syria she received the Heinrich Böll Residency for Writers 2018. She lives in Berlin, Germany.

KATHARINE HALLS is an Arabic-to-English translator from Cardiff, Wales. Her translation of Ahmed Naji's prison memoir *Rotten Evidence* was shortlisted for the National Book Critics Circle Award in autobiography/memoir, and she was awarded a 2021 PEN/Heim Translation Fund Grant to translate Haytham El-Wardany's short story collection *Things That Can't Be Fixed*. Her translation, with Adam Talib, of Raja Alem's *The Dove's Necklace* received the 2017 Sheikh Hamad Award for Translation and was shortlisted for the Saif Ghobash Banipal Prize for Arabic Literary Translation. Her translations for the stage have been performed at the Royal Court and the Edinburgh Festival, and short texts have appeared in *Frieze*, the *Kenyon Review*, *The Believer*, *Africa Is a Country*, *The Common*, *Asymptote*, *Arts of the Working Class*, *World Literature Today*, *Stadtsprachen*, *Words Without Borders*, *Exberliner*, *Newfound*, *Adda*, *Critical Muslim*, *Perpetual Postponement*, and various anthologies.

MAHA HASSAN is among the most prominent Arab novelists of recent years with over eight novels to her name. She is Syrian Kurdish and lives in exile in France. Two of her works were longlisted for the International Prize for Arabic Fiction. She was also awarded the Hellman-Hammett Grant from Human Rights Watch in 2005, as part of a program for persecuted writers. Hassan's work has been translated into several languages, including English, French, Italian, and her native Kurdish. She is yet to have a full-length novel of hers in English translation.

ALICE HOLTTUM is a freelance translator and translation proofreader. She was born in Edinburgh in 1979 and currently resides there, where she also works as a furniture maker. She has a joint honors BA in Russian and Arabic and an MA in applied translation studies (Arabic-English), both from the University of Leeds.

SAWAD HUSSAIN is a translator from Arabic whose work in 2023 was shortlisted for the Warwick Prize for Women in Translation and the Saif Ghobash Banipal Prize for Arabic Literary Translation and longlisted for the Moore Prize for Human Rights Writing. She is a judge for the Palestine Book Awards and the Armory Square Prize for South Asian Literature in Translation. She has run translation workshops under the auspices of Shadow Heroes, Africa Writes, Shubbak Festival, the Yiddish Book Center, the British Library, and the National Centre for Writing.

ELISABETH JAQUETTE is a translator from Arabic and executive director of the American Literary Translators Association. Her translation of *Minor Detail* by Adania Shibli was a finalist for the National Book Awards, and longlisted for the International Booker Prize. Her other translations include *Thirteen Months of Sunrise* by Rania Mamoun, *The Queue* by Basma Abdel Aziz, and *The Frightened Ones* by Dima Wannous.

OMAR AL JBAAI is a writer, actor, theater director, and interactive theater trainer, born on December 12, 1982, in As-Suwayda, Syria. He is a 2006 graduate of the Department of Theatre Studies–Higher Institute of Dramatic Arts in Damascus. He has been a playwright since 2003. In 2021, his play *The Coward* was published by Mamdouh Adwan Publishing House (in Arabic). He was a founding member of Al-Street Workshop for New Playwriting in Damascus in 2007. He has acted since 1997 in several television series and theater performances, the most recent of which was the play *Le Présent qui déborde—Notre Odyssées II*, directed by Christiane Jatahy and produced by the Théâtre National Wallonie-Bruxelles. He was a dramaturg for several theatrical performances, including: *A Thousand and One Tent*, *A Dream*, and *One Word*. He is a trainer and facilitator of group sessions using the techniques of interactive theater and Theater of the Oppressed. His stories, articles, and literary criticism, have been collected in a book entitled *The Land of the Smurfs*, published by Beit Al-Muwatin Publishing in 2018.

MARGARET LITVIN is associate professor of Arabic and comparative literature at Boston University. The author of *Hamlet's Arab Journey: Shakespeare's Prince and Nasser's Ghost* (2011), and the co-editor of *Russian-Arab Worlds: A Documentary History* (2023), her current research aims to reconstruct the literary legacies of Arab writers' ties with Russia and the Soviet Union during the long twentieth century. Her translations from Arabic include Sonallah Ibrahim's 2011 novel *Ice* and several plays, and she was awarded a PEN/Heim Translation Fund Grant to translate Khalil Alrez's *The Russian Quarter*.

ALIA MALEK is a journalist and former civil rights lawyer whose work has appeared in the *New York Times Magazine* and other publications. She is the author of two books: *The Home That Was Our Country: A Memoir of Syria* and *A Country Called Amreeka: US History Retold Through Arab American Lives*. She also served as the editor of *Patriot Acts: Narratives of Post 9/11*

Injustices (Voice of Witness 2011) and *Europa* اپورو أ : *An Illustrated Introduction to Europe for Migrants and Refugees*. She is currently the director of international reporting at the Newmark School of Journalism at the City University of New York.

AHMED NAJI is a bilingual writer, journalist, documentary filmmaker, and official criminal from Egypt. His novels are: *Rogers* (2007), *Using Life* (2014), *And Tigers to My Room* (2020), *Happy Endings* (2023), and most recently a memoir, *Rotten Evidence: Reading and Writing in Prison* (McSweeney's, 2023), which was a finalist at the National Book Critics Circle. He is currently exiled in Las Vegas, Nevada. You can read more about his work at ahmednaji.net.

IBRAHIM SAMU'IL was born in Damascus and graduated from Damascus University's Department of Philosophy and Psychology. He has published four short story collections, *The Smell of the Heavy Footstep*, *Clearings of the Throat*, *Abrupt Blue*, and *The House with the Low Doorway*, and an essay collection, *Paper Spaces*. His work has been translated into French, Italian, Bulgarian, Japanese, and Chinese, and in 2023 he was decorated by Egypt's Diwan al-Arab for his contributions to Arab culture.

SOMAR SHEHADEH, born in 1989 in Latakia, is a Syrian novelist. He is the author of four novels, *Now My Life Begins*,

Yesterday's Houses, *Desertion*, and *Fields of Corn*, and the recipient of several awards, including the al-Tayeb Salih Prize for Literary Creativity (2016) and the Naguib Mahfouz Award for Fiction (2021). Shehadeh also works as a literary editor with a number of Arabic publishing houses and is a weekly columnist for the newspaper *Al-Araby Al-Jadeed*.

RAWAA SONBOL (1979) is a Syrian writer of short fiction, theater, and children's literature. She has published three short story collections: *The Tongue Hunter* (2017), which received the Sharjah Award for Arab Creativity, *The Green Dragon's Wife and Other Colorful Stories* (2019), and most recently *Do, Yek* (2023), which was shortlisted for the 2024 Almultaqa Prize. The stories included in this issue are excerpted from *Do, Yek*, which was first published in the original Arabic by Dar Mamdouh Adwan for Publishing and Distribution. Her writing for the stage and her children's books have also earned her multiple accolades from across the Arab world. She has long been preoccupied with the question of women's self-awareness and has more recently found herself writing about those who have remained in Syria throughout the war. She lives in Damascus where she works as a pharmacist.

ZAKARIA TAMER is a writer from Damascus, Syria. He is one of the most widely read and translated short story writers of modern Syrian literature.

MAISAA TANJOUR is a freelance translator and researcher. She was born in Syria in 1979 and currently resides in Leeds. She is also an interpreter with years of experience working in diverse professional, humanitarian, local and multicultural communities and organizations. Maisaa pursued her education at Al-Baath University, attaining a BA in English language and literature, along with a PG Diploma in literary studies. In 2005, she relocated to the United Kingdom to study at the University of Leeds, achieving an MA in interpreting and translation studies (English-Arabic/Arabic-English), followed by a PhD in translation studies.

DIMA WANNOUS is a Damascus-born novelist. Soon after the Syrian revolution began, Dima was faced with death threats and arrest, which led her to leave the country for Beirut, where she lived for six years. During this time, Dima worked extensively as a journalist as well as a TV anchor on Arab channels. She worked for the prominent *As-Safir* newspaper and hosted a weekly television program on Orient, a Syrian opposition channel, where she interviewed Arab and international political and intellectual figures. It is also while in Beirut that Dima wrote and published her second novel, *The Frightened Ones*, which was shortlisted for the International Prize for Arabic Fiction, also known as the Arabic Booker Prize. The novel was translated into many languages, including English, French, German, Italian, and Dutch. Since 2017, Dima has been living in London, where she pursues her work in journalism and television. Her third novel, *The Family Who Devoured Its Men*, was translated into Portuguese.

MARY WILLIAMS is a Peace Corps volunteer who has served in Uganda and Mexico. She is the author of the memoir *The Lost Daughter* and the children's book *Brothers in Hope*. She has contributed to *McSweeney's Quarterly*, *The Believer*, and *Oprah* magazine.

ODAI AL ZOUBI is a Syrian short story writer, essayist, and translator. He has a PhD in philosophy from the University of East Anglia. His publications include *Half-Smile* (Mamdouh Adwan Publishing House, 2022), *The Book of Wisdom and Naivete* (Mamdouh Adwan Publishing House, 2019), *Windows* (Al-Mutawassit Publications, 2017), and *Silence* (Al-Mutawassit Publications, 2015). You can read his latest essay, "Last Christmas," in English and listen to Bill Nighy reading it on the app Alexander: alxr.com.

MY GAZA: A CITY IN PHOTOGRAPHS
by Jehad al-Saftawi

My Gaza offers a startling perspective on contemporary Gaza. Photographer Jehad al-Saftawi documents his life there up until his escape, in 2016. His eye is drawn to moments of humanity and tenderness that redefine this place beyond propaganda, beyond prevailing narratives. Through vivid images and captions, al-Saftawi exposes a situation that cannot withstand further escalation. Urgent and resolute, *My Gaza* is the first book of its kind, presenting photos of present-day Gaza by a Gazan journalist.

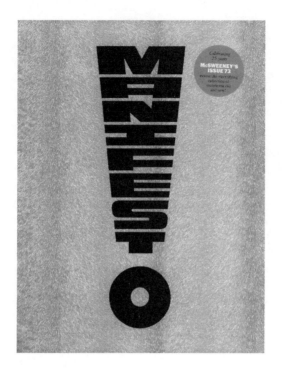

McSWEENEY'S 73: MANIFESTO

A subjective and selective group of manifestos, all from the twentieth century and onward, all roaring with outrage and plans for a better world. Featuring life- and history-changing works from André Breton, Bertrand Russell, Valerie Solanas, Huey Newton, John Lee Clark, Dadaists, Futurists, Communists, Personists, and many more past and future -ists, plus brand-new work from brilliant radical thinkers Eileen Myles and James Hannaham. Let this incendiary collection light your whole world on fire.

ALSO AVAILABLE
FROM McSWEENEY'S

ART AND COMICS

ALL THIS AND MORE AT

STORE.McSWEENEYS.NET

Founded in 1998, McSweeney's is an independent publisher based in San Francisco. McSweeney's exists to champion ambitious and inspired new writing, and to challenge conventional expectations about where it's found, how it looks, and who participates. We're here to discover things we love, help them find their most resplendent form, and place them into the hands of curious, engaged readers.

THERE ARE SEVERAL WAYS TO SUPPORT MCSWEENEY'S:

Support Us on Patreon
visit *www.patreon.com/mcsweeneysinternettendency*

Subscribe & Shop
visit *store.mcsweeneys.net*

Volunteer & Intern
email *eric@mcsweeneys.net*

Sponsor Books & *Quarterlies*
email *amanda@mcsweeneys.net*

To learn more, please visit *www.mcsweeneys.net/donate*
or contact Executive Director Amanda Uhle at
amanda@mcsweeneys.net or 415.642.5609.

McSweeney's Literary Arts Fund is a nonprofit
organization as described by IRS 501(c)(3).
Your support is invaluable to us.